The Culture of the Internet and the Internet as Cult

Social Fears and Religious Fantasies

The Culture of the Internet and the Internet as Cult

Social Fears and Religious Fantasies

By Philippe Breton

Translated by David Bade

Litwin Books, LLC
Duluth, Minnesota

This is a translation of a work by Philippe Breton, titled,

" LE CULTE DE L'INTERNET
Une menace pour le lien social ?"

© Editions LA DÉCOUVERTE, Paris, France, 2000.

Translation and Introduction copyright David Bade, 2010.

Published by Litwin Books, LLC, 2011
PO Box 3320
Duluth, MN 55803

http://litwinbooks.com/

This book is printed on acid-free paper that meets all present ANSI
standards for archival preservation.

Library of Congress Cataloging-in-Publication Data

Breton, Philippe, 1951-
 [Culte de l'Internet. English]
 The culture of the Internet and the Internet as cult : social fears
and religious fantasies / by Philippe Breton ; translated by David
Bade.
     p. cm.
 Includes bibliographical references and index.
 ISBN 978-1-936117-41-3 (alk. paper)
1. Internet--Social aspects. 2. Communication--Social aspects. I.
Title.
 HM851.B7413 2011
 303.48'33--dc22
                                    2010038287

Contents

Philippe Breton:

A brief introduction by the translator

David Bade,
Joseph Regenstein Library
University of Chicago
August 11, 2010

I discovered the work of Philippe Breton when *Le cult de l'Internet: une menace pour le lien social?* arrived in the library in 2000. I read it and immediately ordered everything he had published. I regularly check to see if he has published anything new, and I have his latest book on order at the Seminary Coop Bookstore now: *Le silence et la parole: contre les excès de la communication* (written in collaboration with David Le Breton). Breton's first book, for which he received the Prix de jury from the Association française des informaticiens in 1988, was *Une histoire de l'informatique,* published in 1987. That book was reviewed (along with two other titles on the topic) by I. Bernard Cohen in the journal *Technology and Culture* in 1990;[1] Cohen had little to say about it and nothing good. His

---

[1] Cohen, I. Bernard (1990). [review of A History of Computing Technology. By Michael R. Williams; Prehistoire et histoire des ordinateurs: Origi-

complaint? Breton's history was not the history he had expected, as it dealt not with the details of technical innovations
but with the social, political and ideological views of the men
who made the field and the ethical aspects of their worldview.
Cohen recognized that Breton was writing as a philosopher
rather than an historian of engineering and he wanted nothing to do with philosophy.[2]

Since his history of informatics Breton has written a series
of remarkable books on communication and information
technologies, language, rhetoric, argumentation and the inter-
play among language, technology and ideology in our time.
His thinking from the beginning has joined together the philosophy of information science, the anthropology of language, technologies of communication, and the practices of
rhetoric, argumentation and political communication. His
books have been translated into Arabic, Greek, Hungarian,
Italian, Portuguese, Romanian, Russian, Serbian, Spanish and
Vietnamese, but until now, not into English. In 1991 his anthropological study of the early users of computers, *La tribu
informatique,* received the grand prize for literature in information science, and in 1998 *La parole manipulée* was awarded the
prize for moral and political philosophy of the Académie
française des sciences morale et politiques. I will never forget
reading his *À l'image de l'Homme: du golem aux créatures virtuelles*
(1996): his concluding analysis of the history of projects for
making artificial life and the ideas about what a human being
is that has informed them left me in a state of shock. His
monographs on rhetoric and argumentation made me realize

---

nes du calcul aux premiers calculateurs electroniques. By Robert Ligon-
niere; and Une histoire de l'informatique by Philippe Breton], Technology
and Culture, v. 31, nr. 4, pp. 907-911.
[2] That Breton could have written the book Cohen wanted to read is evident
in the only books of Breton's that I have not read: *L'option informatique au
lycée* and *Pour comprendre l'informatique*, his textbooks of computer science
written for French high school students.

the enormous significance of the absence of argument and debate in a technical system based on rules, algorithms and instructions, for here we enter directly into the political realm. Within information science language is understood to be nothing but information, bits, packets, stuff to send and receive, while the human reality is that language is argument and debate, understanding and misunderstanding, desire and domination. These contrasting visions of communication and language in human social life constitute a crucially important area for research that has hardly been investigated.

In *Le cult de l'Internet: une menace pour le lien social?* Breton looks at the Internet not as a technical system but as a human project, born of social fears and utopian dreams, of mystical desires, religious fantasies, political demands and economic ideologies. How this Internet of the imagination has altered the social reality in which we now live Breton examines through the lens of his earlier works: his analysis of the history of ideas in information science, his anthropological description of computer users and their relationship to their computers, and his remarkable insights into our species' imagination of what it is to be human.

It has puzzled me for a decade now that no notice was taken of this book in the Anglo-American world of library and information science; only one English language periodical published a review.[3] The only other reviews of his books in an English language periodical were the above-mentioned review of *Une histoire de l'informatique* and a review of *L'explosion de la communication* in *Canadian Journal of Communication*.[4] Even though a decade old, *Le culte de l'Internet* has lost none of its relevance and I am delighted that Litwin Books is publishing this translation. I hope there will be more to come.

---

[3] Eric Dupin's review in *World Press Review*, January 2001, v. 48 nr.1 p. 43.
[4] *Canadian Journal of Communication Annual* 1991 v.16, nr.1 p.161-2.

Books by Philippe Breton (arranged chronologically)

Une histoire de l'informatique. Paris: La Découverte, 1987. (reprinted : Seuil, coll. « Points sciences », Paris, 1990)

Les technosciences en question: éléments pour une archéologie du XXe siècle (with Frank Tinland and Alain-Marc Rieu). Paris: Champ Vallon, Seyssel, 1989.

L'explosion de la communication. La naissance d'une nouvelle idéologie (with Serge Proulx). Paris & Montréal: La Découverte & Boréal, 1989. (reprinted: La Découverte/poche, Paris, 1996. Revised edition published in 2002 as: *L'explosion de la communication à l'aube du XXIe siècle*)

La Tribu informatique. Paris : Métaillié, 1990.

L'utopie de la communication. Paris : La Découverte, 1990. (reprinted: La Découverte/poche, Paris, 1997, 2004).

L'option informatique au lycée (with Éric Heilmann and Guislaine Dufour). Paris: Hachette, 1990 (reprinted 1991 and 1998).

Pour comprendre l'informatique (with Ghislaine Dufourd, Eric Heilmann). Paris: Hachette, 1992.

À l'image de l'homme. Du Golem aux créatures virtuelles. Paris: Seuil, 1995 (coll. « Science ouverte »).

L'argumentation dans la communication. Paris: La Découverte, 1996 (coll. « Repères »).

La parole manipulée. Paris : La Découverte, 1998 (reprinted: La Découverte/Poches, Paris, 1999, 2004).

Histoire des théories de l'argumentation (en collaboration avec
    Gilles Gauthier). Paris : La Découverte, 2000 (coll. «
    Repères »).

Le culte de l'Internet: une menace pour le lien social? Paris: La Dé-
    couverte, 2000.

Éloge de la parole. Paris: La Découverte, 2003.

Argumenter en situation difficile. Paris: La Découverte, 2004.

*L'incompétence démocratique: la crise de la parole au cœur du malaise
    (dans la) politique.* Paris: La Découverte, 2006.

Convaincre sans manipuler - Apprendre à argumenter. Paris: La Dé-
    couverte, 2008.

Les refusants: comment refuse-t-on de devenir exécuteur. Paris: La Dé-
    couverte, 2009.

Le silence et la parole contre les excès de la communication (with
    David Le Breton). Toulouse: Érès, 2009.

Breton's blog on the website of *Le Monde:*
http://argumentation.blog.lemonde.fr/

Foreword

Ronald E. Day
School of Library and Information Science,
Indiana University, Bloomington
September 28, 2010

The rhetorical and financial speculative economy of the Internet that arose in the 1990s and crashed in the early 2000s is one of several information society/information ages that have occurred in the 20th century; though, arguably, none had the speculative financial and social power that this one did. As Philippe Breton (in this book) and others have chronicled, the rhetoric of the 'information society' and the 'information age' was linked to several other rhetorical-socio-cultural, economic, and even political assemblages—the British 'third way,' the American (and others') 'new economy,' regulation school post-Fordism, Knowledge Management, earlier post-industrialist discourses (Daniel Bell and others), and, overall, what became known as neo-liberal 'globalism.'

As Breton's book argues, this 'information age' rhetoric and discourse was a religious fervor whose main virtue—particularly in the eyes of those who profited from it—was to promote the infusion of computers and 'information' into all areas of life in the name of bettering the world. Not coincidently, such a discourse in certain geographical areas (e.g.,

San Francisco's Bay Area) also was tied to hyper-inflation in property values, and, throughout the United States, to a stock market bubble and the social devaluation and neglect—following the Reagan era near-destruction—of the industrial, governmental, and service sector working classes. Techno-logical and economic speculative determinisms often go hand in hand, particularly in a financial-led economy. The condi-tions for the last information age in the United States can be found in Reagan, Bush 1, and Clinton era deregulation and their attacks on the welfare state and unionization (i.e., upon the working body).

The appearance of Breton's book in English ten years af-ter its publication in French in 2000 raises several issues. First, it has to be recognized that Breton's *critique* certainly seems to have been an attempt at a timely intervention into the hyper-speculative rhetoric regarding the Internet, linking American so-called 'classical liberal' economic theory (itself politically rightist) and libertarian 'Californian Ideology' (cri-tiqued by Richard Barbrook and Andy Cameron) with French language kin (foremost, Pierre Lévy's works). Such interven-tions at the time were rare enough, particularly in the United States. In retrospect, the appearance of this book both charts the absolute absurdity, self-contradictions, and social violence that made such a discourse on 'the virtual' possible and popu-lar, and provokes questions regarding what remains of such and what has come after.

Perhaps two of the most penetrating critiques that Breton cites belong, not surprisingly, to literary works that precede the information age/society rhetoric and discourses of the recent period. (As Breton points out, the speculative rhetoric of that period was the culmination of a long run up, and as I suggest, it has a long tail.) The examples belong to the sixth chapter of Breton's book and are those of Isaac Asimov's *Naked Sun*, and later in time, J.G. Ballard's short story, 'The Intensive Care Unit,' a short story in which family members whose relations have been only televisually established engage in patricide and matricide when they actually have a bodily meeting. Whereas the writings at the time of the bad *philosophe* Lévy and the self-serving Bill Gates *explained* the information society/age for the perceived masses, it required fiction writers—particularly, skilled and in some ways perverse science fiction writers—to *describe*, based on observations of recent past social psychologies, the psycho- and the 'psychotechno-pathologies' of the present and the future. Characteristically, the displaced Brit, Ballard, pushed to the then seeming limit a description of a society and world in which 'reason' and 'harmony' are expressions of paranoia and violence, all brought to fruition by the ubiquity of communication and capitalist libertarianism and classical liberalism.

The crescendo of Breton's work thus appears in its last chapter in regard to the relation of ubiquitous computer mediated communication (CMC) to the social bond. In Lévy's works, as in so many others of the period, the 'Internet' is, simply, the means to the global village. Read retrospectively, however, CMC appears in some essential aspects nothing less than horrifying. For, technologies, especially information and communication technologies, don't determine futures, but rather, they allow the expression of what is essential to human beings at a period and place to be expressed in the short and long term. The utopian views of those technologies are nothing more than dreams, having reworked given social and personal drives into wish fulfillments. Over time, however, the traumas and violence work themselves out in the social deployment and use of the technologies. As Ballard showed in his book, *Crash*, cars, built for eased transportation, become the expression of desire, *jouissance*, and the destruction of persons and nature as they become faster and bigger. Airplanes that were meant to ferry us across the Atlantic and Pacific now often keep us for days in a steady state of anxiety as we wait to take off or land or even get on a plane because of the crowded air spaces of deregulated commercialized flight. Television and cinema began by transmitting images and now end by transmitting overloaded multimedia affects and eventually immersive actions. Telephones start with a telephonic means of 'reaching out and touching' someone, and they end with our 'hanging on the telephone' all day long and now in whatever circumstances, longing to be touched. Technical devices, thanks to their relentless logic in key social and personal sites, turn into technologies of pathologies (which were originally the 'unconscious' of their desired invention).

Thus, too, the Internet well serves both the 'long-tail' of desire and memory (particularly in its commodity forms) and the 'short-tail' of paranoia and narcissism. Whereas the easy to read and elegiac futurisms of Gates, Lévy, and others assured us of the future, it is in the punctuated and even ranting *critiques* into the mass of elegiac, but self-contradictory, claims of these discourses that one finds the starting point to an awareness of the real.

As Ballard's short story indicates and as Breton's piece leads up to in its culmination upon the problem of the social bond, not surprisingly the critical understanding of CMC is less purely technological and more psychological. (It is for this reason that rhetorical, financial, and technological economies were so tightly tied together during this most recent 'information age' and why these information ages tend to appear and disappear, erasing behind them their own historical traces.)

CMC has evolved and continues to evolve as a highly mobile, fragmented, means of forming and denying the social bond, across virtual or distant, and local relations, respectively. As Breton highlights, the 'denial of the body' and the celebration of the virtual and the 'post-human' in the discourses that he critiques are a continuing challenge to humanist notions of personal and social being. Indeed, perhaps in this 'all too human' picture, we see the traces of our own animality: CMC affords an unprecedented amount of dalliance and tribalism and a denial of the Sartrean 'hell' of other people in face to face contact. In CMC, 'the representational animal' of today has found a way to live with itself and others. Here, too, at least in the United States today—echoing the development and use of radio and television in the U.S. and Europe early in the 20th century (e.g., Weimar Germany)—, factionalism and extremisms become more powerful, though the governing ideology remains intact and actually drives these to greater expressive force. The limits upon the ego are protected and released in the plethora and reach of CMC.

This, to my mind at least, is what Breton's book leads up to: the problem of the relation of CMC to a social logic of paranoia and narcissism that is at the core of the logic of capitalism. As Breton indicates, and as the entire discursive and practical social informatics (i.e., Knowledge Management, 'New Economy,' etc.) of the recent information age shows, CMC has developed along the lines of a social psychology of agony. That agony is the need for social touch within a moral logic, politics, and psychology of capitalism. The end result is a deferment of the social bond to the furthest regions of the networked earth, and as the popular info-lit suggests, to the ends of thought (even divorced from the body).

Certainly, the picture of the Internet here is neither utopian nor dystopian. It is a realist picture akin to those works of Ballard's compatriot, the painter Francis Bacon, where the body melts out through the pathological extension of certain materially leveraged all-too-human traits. The subject's liquefied flesh hangs off the body, thanks to the technology of communication—in Bacon's works, paint, in CMC, transmitted words.

All of this, of course, does not address the tremendous good that networked communication can provide for research communities, scholarship, learning, distant friendships and communities, and even—hopefully—for the continuation of us along with those non-human animals whose presence on the Internet seems more than any other thing to be depictive. Such, however, is neither Breton's scope nor is it the scope of the psychological pathology of the 'information age' and the 'information society.' The demarcation of the limits of the real, the symbolic, and the imaginary in regard to technologies is very difficult to do, not the least because such questions are further inflected through specific groups and individuals. In this way, there is in reality no 'Internet.' But, in modernity we have been and still are very much shaped and governed by larger ideological and economic tropes and mechanisms, as well. It is the critique of these that still very much escapes the 'positivism' of the age, in every sense of the term. It is into the psychological and ideological-technical 'bubble' of the recent past and still remaining present information age that Breton's book bravely dives and engages.

Introduction

Anyone who reads the press, listens to the radio or watches television, anyone who consults the numerous articles and works dedicated to the "new information technologies," the "global information society," and "cyberspace" may reasonably ask the question: Has the Internet—and everything which is associated with it: multimedia, computers, informatics, information (in the broadest sense)—become the object of a genuine cult? The unprecedented value placed on everything that touches on the Internet is nothing less than the promise of a better world.

The expression "cult" may be understood in two ways. In the strict sense, a cult is associated with a religious movement that is at the same time both homage given to a divinity and a collection of practices that realize that worship. In a metaphorical sense, a cult is the veneration or simply the strong attachment that one may have for anything or anyone.

In the beginning of this enquiry the use of the phrase "cult of the Internet"[5] represents a simple metaphor. An

---

[5] According to usage, the word Internet is sometimes accompanied by an article (the Internet). This usage is common among the true pioneers of the global network, but also among some of those more recently converted who wish to demonstrate in this manner that they are not ignorant of the heroic character of its birth and of the revolution that it represents for all of humanity. Throughout this book we have chosen not to use the honorific article, though more and more often it is found in this way in the printed or "on-line" press. To our eyes, "Internet" is a common noun that

American author, Theodore Roszak, used the term "cult" in his description of the constellation of attitudes and beliefs that accompanied the origins of microcomputing.[6] Yet as this book progresses the metaphor draws closer to the strict sense: the infatuation for the Internet displays itself in a climate that has all the appearance of a new religiosity. The closer one approaches the milieu of the most ardent proselytes, the more clearly this religiosity appears.

The idea that behind the most radical discourses regarding the Internet there must be a religious phenomenon in the strict sense has already been glimpsed by many authors. Pierre Musso came close when he wove a genealogy of the Internet that pointed to the "philosophy of the network of Saint-Simon,"[7] the famous French engineer of the nineteenth century, founder of a "universal religion of communication," of a "new Christianity."

Armand Mattelart evokes the question as well when he writes of the religious dimension present in Marshall McLuhan, the advocate of the "global village" and one of the spiritual fathers of the Internet.[8] In his global analysis of the phenomena of communication, Ignacio Ramonet foresaw a possible "messianism of media" including the new information

---

designates a simple tool (even though it is still written with an initial upper case letter). On the other hand we have deliberately used the article in the title of the book in order to indicate the religious dimension that bathes the thoroughfares of the Internet (on questions of vocabulary, see the lucid and humorous analysis of Alain Le Diberder: *Histoire d'@: Abécédaire du cyber*, La Découverte, Paris, 2000). [Translators' note: In this translation the presence or absence of the definite article follows English usage; the author's distinction has not been maintained.]

[6] Theodore Roszak, *The Cult of Information*, Pantheon, New York, 1986.

[7] Pierre Musso, *Télécommunications et philosophie des réseaux. La postérité paradoxale de Saint-Simon*, PUF, Paris, 1997.

[8] Armand Mattelart, *Histoire de l'utopie planétaire. De la cité prophétique à la société globale*, La Découverte, Paris, 1999.

technologies.[9] David Le Breton has laid the foundations for a
path linking ancient Gnosticism to the religiosity of cyberculture.[10] And finally, Mark Dery recalls the importance of New
Age religiosity for American cyberculture.[11] Many others
share this same intuition.

Still, one must press the enquiry further and restrict the
metaphor in order to see if the cult of the Internet does not
mask a more profound anthropological reality, the beginning,
perhaps, of a reconstitution of religious feeling in the decades
to come. A few years ago we proposed an anthropological
approach to the "information tribe" based on fieldwork.[12]
Our current enquiry is a continuation of that first voyage
through the world of the new technologies and attempts to
hone in on the deep beliefs buried in the heart of the Internet
which ultimately give it its meaning.

From this point of view, *World philosophie*, the work of the
philosopher Pierre Lévy on this subject,[13] with its profoundly
mystical and prophetic accents, constitutes a valuable guide
for introducing us to this new dimension. If this work is cited
often in the book it is because it expresses the strongest formulation of the dimension of latent religiosity that permeates
the Internet milieu. It is appropriate to give him so much
space, as he is the theologian most engaged with the "new
world."

It is equally necessary to take a historical approach, for
this also permits us to sort out the effects of fashion and im-
mediacy that so often characterize approaches to this milieu.
The Internet was not born in a day and is, after all, no more

---

[9] Ignacio Ramonet, *La tyrannie de la communication*, Galilée, Paris, 1999.

[10] David Le Breton, *L'adieu au corps*, Métailié, Paris, 1999.

[11] Mark Dery, *Vitesse virtuelle. La cyberculture aujourd'hui*, Abbeville, Paris, 1997.

[12] Philippe Breton, *La tribu informatique. Enquête sur une passion moderne*, Métailié, Paris, 1990.

[13] Pierre Lévy, *World philosophie*, Odile Jacob, Paris, 2000.

than a branch of a larger cult, that of information, born in the heart of the visions of "cybernetics" in the forties.

This new religiosity is not a religion. The reader must not expect to find here a body of doctrines that will have the familiar allure for those who are habituated to the mysteries of monotheistic influences. The rigorous theologies and complete symbolic systems to which those have given birth since Moses are not found here. There is indeed a rupture with monotheism.

Still in formation, this new religiosity is above all a nebula; homogeneity is not its principal characteristic. It is diffuse, for it is a religiosity of the dispersed, the splintered, the uncentered. Our enquiry has only been more difficult because of that. It opens up paths which have been sketched only in part. Some are perhaps blind alleys or illusions. In spite of all that, we have attempted to extract a solid core of faith held by those whom we have called the "fundamentalists of the Internet."

The borrowings and supports which that new religiosity finds in ancient religious currents such as Gnosticism and Puritanism, from more recent imports from the Far East such as Buddhism, and from the marginally religious movements like free-market capitalism, prevent the exact nature of that religiosity from appearing to come from a sociologically clearly identifiable "center."

What is the object of this cult? The point of departure is the sharing of a common vision that has been progressively refined and developed in the context of the new technologies and beyond. That vision is of an ideal world that would be composed entirely of form, behavior, information, message, communication; a world made of elements constantly in movement, in change, in interaction. For this cult, the world is a world comprised entirely of relations. In such a world, everything would be pure communication. Everything would be, as Norbert Wiener, the founder of cybernetics wrote, "flame and whirlwind" rather than vile matter, spirit rather than body.

It presents a mystique of form and message that mobilizes the same affective resources that are put into the service of established religions. It is perhaps the spirituality of the third millennium. In it, information is the true value, the true nature of things, and thus must we regard matters if we wish to understand the real.

According to this vision, when the movement of information slows, Evil lies waiting: entropy, censorship, borders, closure, law, interiority, materiality, centrality, individuality, the body. It suggests an imperative of continuous communication, the most rapid possible.

The promise of this new vision is a better world, a New Jerusalem: everything is consciousness, spirit, virtuality. It is also the promise of a better human being with an enlarged consciousness, since it will be rooted in a collective consciousness united with intelligent machines. Fashioned by a desire for non-violence at the same time Eastern and resonating powerfully in the heart of North American culture, the Internet is also the bearer of the utopia of a pacified society. The price to be paid—we shall analyze it at length—is physical separation, the end of direct encounter. These conditions, draconian, almost monastic, nourish the ideal of a new social bond, entirely virtual—that is, spiritual—where, in order to be reunited in a new communion, we must initially separate ourselves from one another.

In order to commune it is necessary to communicate, and in order to communicate it is necessary to be separated. Here we arrive at the heart of a new transcendence which is certainly not a belief in God (in this sense also it is not a matter of a deism) but which has on the other hand a very precise idea of Evil and of violence, where the enfeeblement of monotheism is accompanied by an increasingly dramatic presence of "the two," as Denis Duclos has shown.[14]

The influence of Teilhard de Chardin is not far off: he defined the "noosphere" as a "net of psychic energy" that spreads over the earth in proportion as Man takes possession; he also saw the future of humanity as a new "collectivism."

The cult organizes itself around all the practices that allow the activation of forms, putting information in movement, promotion of openness and transparency, favoring all instances of communication. By a curious inversion, the content of communication becomes secondary, a simple pretext for the activation of forms. "One must communicate" is the main injunction that defines the spaces of the new rites.

The Internet is the true Church for those who venerate information. The networks, the computers, all of the communication devices become so many privileged, almost exclusive places where the new cult is practiced. They render obsolete the "old," "archaic" forms of communication, of mediation, of knowing, of leisure and, in general, of contact with others.

The cultic is always near to the cultural. It is established through practices where each gesture is significant, where the difference between the sacred and the profane is effaced along with an increase of energies expended in daily haste throughout the whole of life. The cult of the Internet implies a new relation to the social bond. It implies living in a certain manner in which communication should never cease but on the contrary may culminate in the eventual attainment of a point of almost mystical exaltation. The new religiosity assumes the possibility of an ecstasy of communication.

---

[14] Denys Duclos, *Le complexe du loup-garou. la fascination de la violence dans la culture américaine*, La Découverte, Paris, 1994 (édition de poche: Pocket, Paris, 1999).

Certainly all the internauts who use the Internet for its evident functionalities such as e-mail do not share the purposes of the Internet fundamentalists. These latter are no less at the center of the plan for not being its creators. Their influence is immense since it is they who actually give meaning and direction to a "technological macrosystem,"[15] the uses of which politicians did not discover until very late.

The new religiosity that surrounds the Internet has recently been publicly displayed with the theme, so popular in certain circles, of the "global information society." In this domain the new Church is not separated from the State. Is not the real question less one of technology than of symbolism, politics, and more concretely, of the social bond? Will the "utopia of an asocial society," where "cyberspace" remains as the only support for the social bond, be imposed upon us by this bias, as French university collaborator with *Le Monde diplomatique* Asdrad Torres thinks?

Our enquiry will not be satisfied with merely bringing to light a core of little known mystical illumination. We shall also bring to light the points of opposition and antagonism with which the new faith collides. As the new religiosity is not far from being considered by some as a heresy in regard to both humanism and monotheism, so it is opposed, point by point, to these two pillars of our "old" cultures.

Are we not headed for a new, original and unexpected form of normative collectivism tied to the universalizing constraints of the methods of information technologies? Does this collectivism under the form of the "global reconnection of the human species with itself"[16] as Pierre Lévy likes to call it, not risk realization at the cost of the loss of everything

---

[15] On this notion, see Alain Gras, *Grandeur et dépendance, sociologie des macrosystèmes techniques*, with the participation of Sophie L. Poirot-Delpech, PUF, Paris, 1993.

[16] Pierre Lévy, *World philosophie, op. cit.*, p. 20.

dependent on the body, of interiority, of memory, of expression, of the capacity for argument, of direct communication,
in short, of our essential humanity?

With these new information technologies in the service of
building a new "tower of Babel" is there not, as Shmuel
Trigano believes, a new risk of massification, where "man will
lose his image," his individuality?[17] Does the new cult of the
virtual signify that "goodbye to the body" must be the foundation of human identity, a farewell that David Le Breton so
forcefully decries and denounces?[18]

We shall see that we are very far—at least from the point
of view we are defending—from the radiant promises of a
better world for all. The "Internet-for-everything"[19]—the
option of developing the Internet wherever it is technically
possible—entails many grave risks for the social bond. The
worst of these risks is without doubt that even if the utopia
of a global information society is not realized, a certain form
of devaluation of the social bond and the human person will
make its way into that plan which governs our destinies, the
symbols by which we live.

Does not the image of a human being without an interior,
purged of the memory and interiority that constitutes human
individuality, risk imposing itself and nourishing other utopias, such as "perfect health," the potential for which Lucien
Sfez denounces?[20]

Where did this new cult come from? What are its historical roots? Why has it apparently met with such great success?
Can one know if its promises will be fulfilled? If this new
world should be imposed, is there not a major risk for an al-

---

[17] Shmuel Trigano, *Le monothéisme est un humanisme*, Odile Jacob, Paris, 2000.
[18] David Le Breton, *L'adieu au corps, op. cit.*
[19] Translators' note: The author uses the phrase "tout-Internet"; the immediately following definition which he offers makes clear the meaning of the
phrase as he intends it.
[20] Lucien Sfez, *La santé parfaite*, Le Seuil, Paris, 1995.

ready fragile social bond? Will the new "global information society" reduce itself to a strictly collectivist universe, where the individual will be condemned to isolation after all? These are the questions that this work poses, refusing the false alternative "for or against the Internet" but giving voice to those who plead, far from all fetishism, for a human use of technology, in sum, for a *secularization* of communication.

1.

For or against the Internet:
A false alternative

Despite the intense publicity that the Internet receives and the extreme value given to the new information technologies today, opinion on this theme is far from unanimous. Many remain silent in the public forum, notably those who refuse on principle to repeat the innumerable commonplaces that often form the main substance of what the Internet is understood to be. Nevertheless, they think about it.

One may distinguish three positions *grosso modo*: first the "Internet-for-everything" militants, proselytes (sometimes unknowingly) of a new cult. Then there are the technophobes, hostile to all technology. Finally, there are those who think that a rational use of technology may under certain conditions be a factor of progress. Those who take the first attitude appear to be the majority, and their point of view tends to become the "dominant ideology" in this area, the only possible and legitimate manner of regarding the question, to the point that they often cannot even imagine that there could be any other. Those with the second attitude are more numerous than they appear. Through philosophy, ignorance or simply irritation, with a sort of passive resistance, underground but effective, they oppose the diffusion of the new information technologies. The third position, held by those who tend to take a measured view of technology, is still largely undeveloped. Such a position is often formed of mul-

tiple experiences that are difficult to unify. It rests on humanist values that are difficult to affirm, and of which some are
today in crisis.

The advocates of "Internet-for-everything"

The first position is defended by those who employ all
their energy in developing the Internet and trying to apply it
to every aspect of our lives, private, public and professional.
These are the prophets of "Internet-for-everything." They
have only one vision of the future: a world in which the new
information technologies will be the new center, an invasive
center since it will be everywhere. In this circle, the Internet is
the object of a true cult. One member of this circle enthusias-
tically wrote,

> Cosmic history [...] has a direction, it possesses a completely
> discernable meaning, which is the intensification of the vir-
> tual character of the world. [...] The borders of the world
> will become more permeable, malleable, interactive, they will
> burgeon in every sense. Cosmic and cultural evolution today
> culminate in the virtual world of cyberspace."[21]

They do not hesitate to speak of a "new world" which
they oppose to the old world that will disappear. This virtual
world, that of the network, also called "cyberspace" due to its
origin in cybernetics, will progressively displace the archaic
"real world." Even so, the "Internet-for-everything" is defended by attaching it to many sensibilities. At the center, one
finds those who often have a prophetic style and give the
movement its meaning. It is often from among intellectuals
of the lineage of McLuhan that the militants of the information society, and now the Internet, have arisen. Their position
is impregnated with religiosity. Among those in this camp
one finds the Frenchmen Pierre Lévy and Philippe Quéau. It

---

[21] Pierre Lévy, World philosophie, op. cit., p. 160.

is among the ranks of these intellectuals that one finds the fundamentalists of the Internet.

Pierre Lévy is the author of a number of works in which mystical accents are increasingly evident. His influence on the Internet milieu is important. His last book, a passionate argument in favor of a "world philosophy"[22] is a good synthesis of certain attitudes of that milieu. The other author mentioned above, Philippe Quéau, has the support of his position as director of the informatics and information division of UNESCO in his attempts to convince the fools who "still have not seen" that a "new metaphysical revolution" is in progress, where "the real becomes completely language," therefore information, and where, thanks to cyberspace, "a perfect identity of map and territory" will be achieved.[23]

These two authors crystallize the general thinking found in new information technology circles, by those who often see themselves as the bearers of values and a mission vis-à-vis the rest of humanity. If all the enthusiastic advocates of the Internet do not feel themselves invested with such prophetic visions, these two nonetheless offer a philosophical background accepted and assumed by many, in more or less vulgarized forms. They constitute the "Internet worldview."

Many of the advocates of this new cult are convinced in every way that these technologies are by nature bringers of progress and that the more our world commits itself to new information technologies, the better it will be. Many information scientists subscribe to this view. Thus the American, Nicholas Negroponte, is the author of a celebrated book on "being digital" in which he defends the idea that "informatics is a way of life" in which the ideal is henceforth to be able "to

---

[22] *Ibid.*

[23] Remarks by Philippe Quéau at the colloquium "De Gutenberg ao terceiro milénio," Universidad autonoma de Lisboa, 6-8 avril 2000.

meet one's neighbor in the realm of number."[24] Robert Caillau, information scientist at CERN (Centre européen de re-
cherches nucléaires), in Geneva, and one of the principal in-
ventors of the "Web," also claims that "the computer is not a
machine," and that after the culture of the hunt and physical
force, of agriculture and money, will come the world of networks and information.[25] Bill Gates, the very mediatized
founder of Microsoft, old libertarian and neo-liberal, ardently
defends a world in which information absorbs all our activities.

Besides the prophets and the technicians, one finds all
those who, for one reason or another, have an interest—or
believe they have an interest—in the development of the Internet-for-everything. This is notably the case of the gurus of
the "new economy," who see in the maximum development
of the network the occasion to multiply profits or even rapidly build fortunes. This is also the case with politicians, often
surrounded by ardent counselors on these matters, who feel it
is an occasion to fulfill their political program by riding a
wave that they judge to be popular. In particular, one thinks
of the American vice-president Al Gore, or of all those like
Lionel Jospin in France who are tempted by a "society of
information solidarity."

Most of all, the Internet can be a formidable career accel-
erator. Whatever they do or do not believe, a certain number
of persons ardently campaign in favor of overthrowing the
values of our society and a rapid passage to a "global information society" regardless of the consequences, provided that
it serves their individual destinies. How many have also made
a rapid career by being led voluntarily, by an enterprise or an
institution, to develop the new tool for those who little un-

---

[24] Nicholas Negroponte, *Being Digital*, Knopf, New York, 1995.
[25] Remarks by Robert Caillau at the colloquium "De Gutenberg ao terceiro
milénio," Universidad autonoma de Lisboa, 6-8 avril 2000.

derstand it or mistrust it? Not everyone has done a bad job, but since the power that they can attain is proportionate to the importance of the place in things that the tool attains, the temptation to find oneself an advocate of the Internet-for-everything is strong.

Prophets, technological optimists, or simply professionals driven by the Internet, all understand and mutually support one another in order to bring about a new "revolution," hardly ever asking themselves about the social and human consequences of such a faith. These people find the justification for their real life actions in the writings of the "prophets" of the global information society who proclaim the arrival of a "new world," and these latter support their remarks with the many examples taken "from real life."

The technophobes

Nowadays it is difficult to oppose the spread of the wave of technology and above all the dominant values accompanying it. Yet we would be wrong to believe whatever is unanimously accepted. These values (which we shall analyze in greater detail later) rouse numerous and varied resistances, and there is certainly a technophobic current running through our societies. For some, technology was represented early on as the equivalent of sin. Very often this opposition is supported by religious values or at least an interpretation of those values.

As soon as the idea of the technological society of communication was imagined, notably by the American mathematician Norbert Wiener in a work to which we will return, philosophers such as Jacques Ellul, well known throughout the Protestant world and beyond, have engaged in radical critiques of technology. Ellul's book, *The Technological Society*, was first published in 1947, and was immediately successful, especially in the United States.[26] Since then, Ellul has influenced a whole school of thinkers on technology, one of whom is André Vitalis, who has long worked for the *Commission nationale informatique et libertés.*

In a reflection on monotheism, Shmuel Trigano opposes the "unified and unique world to the 'global village' which is put into place through information systems and the economy," and which "destabilizes the practical framework of human identity."[27] Less important, but comprising nonetheless a rather troublesome light cavalry, are essayists like Paul Virilio, much publicized in the crenels of the radical opposition to the Internet, who warn against the risks of "information Chernobyls" and against a society which is heading ever more quickly towards disaster."[28]

Each in their own way, these positions nourish a necessary debate on the social stakes of the new information technologies. Still another technophobic current exists with a quite different sensibility. It is linked to ignorance and frustration and is essentially found among those who are strangers in the world of technology. This current frequently refers to the inequality of personal and professional situations in a society where technical education is even more difficult to come by than a general education. To widespread illiteracy even at the heart of the richest societies is added "electronic illiteracy," a source of frustration, rejection and hostility.

Against the cult of the Internet, one can distinguish the technophobes of reaction and those of irritation. These two tendencies—both often failing to imagine another discourse

---

[26] Jacques Ellul, *La technique ou l'enjeu du siècle,* Armand Colin, Paris, 1954; *Le bluff technologique*, Hachette, Paris, 1988. English translations: *The Technological Society*, Knopf, New York, 1964; *The Technological Bluff,* Eerdmans, Grand Rapids, 1990.

[27] Shmuel Trigano, *Le monothéisme est un humanisme, op. cit.*

[28] Paul Virilio, *L'art du moteur*, Galilée, Paris, 1993. [English translation: *The Art of the Motor*, Minneapolis, 1995.]

or an alternative to "Internet-for-everything"—toss the baby out with the bathwater and reject the Internet entirely. Their technophobia is more a symptom of the absence of debate on the subject than true hostility to technology.

The advocates of rational use

Between technophiles and technophobes a third way is possible. Regularly during the second half of the twentieth century and throughout the history of the development of the new technologies, voices have arisen to criticize too great an enthusiasm as well as too great a pessimism. Norbert Wiener himself, after having contributed so much, in his own words, to "liberating the bad genie from the bottle," in the 1960s, at the end of his life, made a leap towards humanism.

In the world of informatics some of the most important names have spoken out in favor of a reasoned, humanist use of information technologies and against the mad rush and excess to which those technologies led. As early as the "information revolution" of the sixties and seventies, when a better world through computers was promised, one of the most important researchers in artificial intelligence, the American Joseph Weizenbaum, questioned the complete power accorded to computers in our societies.[29] In France, Jacques Arsac, holder of the first chair of informatics in the faculty of sciences in Paris, took up his pen in 1968 to denounce the attitude that informatics has anything to do with "meaning": for him, that discipline, which he knew well, had to be restricted to the "treatment of form."[30] His position, even though it was not so explicitly stated, was inspired by a religious point of view; his Catholicism would hardly accept

[29] Joseph Weizenbaum, *Computer Power and Human Reason: from Judgment to Calculation*, W.F. Freeman & Co., San Francisco, 1976.
[30] Jacques Arsac, *Les machines à penser*, Seuil, Paris, 1987.

that the realm of meaning proper to the spiritual world should be invested in technology.

For these two specialists, the cause is understood: tools are just tools; all incursion into other domains such as the pretension to make a lever for "social revolution" goes contrary to the humanist ideas which place man—and not technology—at the center of the world. The critique of the "ideology of communication" urged by Lucien Sfez,[31] and the analysis of the "utopia of communication"[32] already carried, each in its own manner, the seeds of a reflection on the reasoned use of technology in a context already largely technologized.

In spite of their own presuppositions, the current "antiglobalization classical liberals" appearing in Europe and elsewhere in the late 1990s contain a potential rational critique of the Internet. In France, the movement spurred on by *Le Monde diplomatique* and its network of friends played an important role in contesting the Internet, perceived by some classical liberals to be an entirely instrumentalized tool. This point of view, expressed for example by Ignacio Ramonet in *La tyrannie de la communication*[33] permits the analysis of the discourse accompanying the new information technologies to be in harmony with the philosophy of European liberalism.

According to another perspective, the partisans of "regulation" of the Internet—juridical and otherwise—played a great role in defense of the controlled usage of the new technologies. This is the meaning of the remarks by the French media sociologist Dominique Wolton who, in *Internet et après?*, tried to restrict the reach of the new technologies and argued

---

[31] Lucien Sfez, *Critique de la communication*, Seuil, Paris, 1988.

[32] Philippe Breton, *L'utopie de la communication*, La Découverte/Poche, Paris, 1997.

[33] Ignacio Ramonet, *op. cit.*

for their regulation, "so that the freedom of communication may not become synonymous with the law of the jungle."[34]

Among the most active partisans of "reasoned usage" today, especially in France, are people involved with teaching. This is undoubtedly why they have been made the butt of irony, even slander, from the most heated advocates of the information society; they are reproached for their apparently well known "resistance to change." It must be admitted that they are not well disposed to it. Since the sixties the information scientists of IBM, promoters of new "pedagogies" of mostly compartmentalized inspiration, confidently announced the end of "human" teachers and their impending replacement by "teaching machines"! This is the same discourse one sometimes finds today, where the Internet, allowing "access to the world's knowledge," dispenses with human mediation, reducing it for the first time to a lesser position, making the professor the students' "assistant." Such an attitude hardly predisposes one to accepting the new technologies. Nevertheless, many teachers have attempted a pedagogical reflection on the rational use in the service of pedagogy and of the necessary teacher-student relation (we shall return to the arguments later).

In the current climate, the advocates of rational use meet in every case with a strong tendency, that of "the Internet-for-everything," and the cult which permeates it. Whatever their points of view or motivations may be, their position in effect implies a partial renunciation of the power of technology and the establishment of strict borders between the world of technology and that of the human. They extol, in a fashion, the inverse of the religiosity that bathes the Internet world: a "lay" usage of technology, a sort of separation of the Church of Technology and the Human State. That explains

[34] Dominique Wolton, *Internet et après? Une théorie critique des nouveaux médias*, Flammarion, Paris, 2000.

why they have the greatest difficulty in leaving their isolation and sharing their experiences. In the face of very strong social pressure, their actions are often confined to something quasi-clandestine.

The difficulties of this "third way" are such that, in spite of strengthening certain intellectuals little suspected of hostility to technology, every critical position or even a simple call for debate about the Internet and the discourse that flatters it is reduced more often than not by the media to the second term of a terribly simplified "for or against." How often it is said to those who express any kind of reservation regarding the "Internet-for-everything": "But that is so bizarre; you use e-mail all the time!" The cult of the Internet is so widespread that many cannot imagine that the Internet could serve simply as... a tool. There is certainly a place for critique, but it is clearly demarcated within the boundaries of what appears to be a false debate: either you are a "technophobe," i.e. one who loves neither technology nor change nor anything modern, or else you are entirely "in favor of the Internet." Either you are closed up within yourself or you are open to the world and its fantastic new world of technology. Either you are "young" advocates of the "new world," or you are "an old poker."

Technophile or technophobe: these are the only positions allowed in the discussion. Such a simplification obviously cannot pretend to have the status of social debate. There are many other trails to blaze toward the beginnings of a "laicization" of technology, paths that are at an equal distance from the quasi-religious ideas with which technologies are often ridiculously clothed and the hostility that is provoked in response. In order to leave behind this false debate it is necessary to better understand the position of the advocates of "Internet-for-everything." What are their arguments? How does their discourse spread? What are the underlying values? Why speak of a "cult"? The following chapters attempt to bring to light what is sometimes only implicit in the discourses that exalt the new information technologies. We begin with that recent favorite of the Internet cult: the promise of a better world thanks to the establishment of a global information society.

2.

The promise of a better world

The second half of the twentieth century witnessed the rise of a new kind of promise, new at least in appearance. That promise right away took on a global, even cosmic dimension. In the beginning, a "world state" was spoken of, then, a "global village." Following that, after the evocation of a "machine to govern the world," there came the era of the "information revolution," which would completely change all of society. The impact on the political lexicon of the term "revolution" still has not peaked. It refers to a changing world, made to turn about on itself, thanks to the new information technologies which began to invade our environment. Some popular writers have not hesitated to speak of the "digital era," to designate that which to their eyes would be a veritable change of civilization. Next they spoke of a vast global network brought about to "change our lives." The word "Internet" succeeded the trivial term "information highway." Then "Cyberspace," a virtual world that was opposed to the "material" world, made its appearance.

Behind all these projects, of which some are beginning to be realized, one finds the same promise, bathed in religiosity, of a "better world" on Earth, of a world where a "new harmony" would be realized by a human community finally reconciled to itself. Some authors transformed themselves into prophets; some gurus converted to the new faith. The cult of the Internet was added to the new and very real communication tools that have come into being as a result of the invention of the computer in June 1945.

The promise of a new life

For those who had navigated the ocean of pessimism regarding the material world, a new shore finally appeared on the horizon, a new world, a "new frontier," as the Americans say. Henceforth everything that the public would hear about the new technologies—mobile phones, for example—would be systematically associated with a whole set of positive values. The new technologies: they bring "more freedom, more employment, more wealth, more democracy, more knowledge." This is the promise, in short, of a world at once different and better over all.

As if in echo to the bad new realities of the real, material world, the plans for a virtual world where everything will be easier and where the presence of others will weigh less heavily on our individual destinies became the archetype of all comments on the subject. Advertisements for the Internet and the mobile phone systematically present us with the same idyllic tableaux, in several similar variants, of persons alone with a vaguely ecstatic air. Often they are flying with ease through the air. They inhabit a transparent world, living carefree ever after. They are alone, but at the same time the promise of the group is there, in a strange form which we shall analyze, as for example this slogan which appeared in the center two pages of a major daily advertising a new "portal" to the Internet with the announcement: "I am what I know, what I feel, what I shall be. I am millions of people and all together we are the Internet."[35]

---

[35] *Le Monde*, July 1, 2000, p 18-19.

The political appropriation

Advertising is only the most visible, spectacular and everyday phase of this promise. It is its imaginary wardrobe. The promise is embodied in more argued fashion in the political discourse of the governments of various nations. The political world is rapidly being taken by this theme, and the majority of people are at first made aware of the promises associated with the new information technologies through the intermediary of the theme of the "global information society," which is spread through various political appeals. The end of the nineties saw a veritable epidemic of government reports on this theme. They had at the same time a concrete, realist dimension, and visionary accents which led them to speak of a "new world." Everything took place as if the habitual register of the political promise had been amplified by the spirit of a new vision.

In 1996, the German government offered its reflections in a first report, entitled, *Info 2000*. The same year, the English experts fought for an "Information Society Initiative." A little earlier in France, Gérard Théry offered to the Prime Minister his report, *Les autoroutes de l'information*, following a request by an interministerial committee held the 22nd of February, 1994. All of these texts differ but little from the "Bangemann report," so-called after the name of its author, the European Commissioner, entitled *L'Europe et la société de l'information planétaire*, issued in May 1994. (Bangemann brought attention to himself in 1998 by resigning from the Commission to take employment in the private telecommunications industry, in contempt of the ethical rules of the Commission.) Far from being the work of independent experts or research specialists on these questions, his report was the fruit of the reflections of persons from the world of the telecommunications and media industries themselves much influenced by the belief that the Internet represented an overthrowing of both the direction of life and our ways of living.

At the same time, and in the same spirit, the Japanese government defined a strategy looking towards the development of information superhighways. Two governmental reports established the framework. The first, edited by Fumio Watanabe, was ambitiously entitled *Reforms toward the Intellectually Creative Society of the 21st Century,* and the second, more concrete, argued in favor of a *Program for Advanced Information Infrastructure.* The Japanese press spoke on that occasion of the construction of a "telematic state," of "infotopia" or of an "information utopia."[36]

The market-oriented pragmatism of all these experts' reports did not exclude a certain lyricism in the exposition of their themes. Thus, on the 7th of December 1994, at the conclusion of a colloquium organized by the Ministry of Industry on this subject, the French Prime Minister Edouard Balladur announced:

> The information superhighway may be one of the stars which, though not giving modern life all its significance, orients it differently. [...] Like these new frontiers that humanity has now given itself as goals to conquer, they can rally enthusiasm, mobilize us and gather our energies together.[37]

The theme of the information society traverses political lines and easily adapts itself to changes in government. One of the very first speeches of Lionel Jospin, who became head of the government of France in June 1997, brought up this question. He demonstrated the will to give the "information society" high priority in government policy even though this

---

[36] Ozaki Takeshi, in an article in *Nihon Keizai Shimbun,* reprinted in the weekly *Courrier International,* no. 195, July 1994.

[37] Cited by Thierry Vedel, "Les politiques des autoroutes de l'information dans les pays industrialisés: une analyse comparative," *Réseaux,* no 78, CNET, 1996, p. 11-25.

theme had not been at the heart of the election campaign. The speech was given before a circle of communications professionals, but its import was national. The media largely echoed the opinions and decisions announced in that speech. Jospin also made a promise there: "The development of the new information and communications networks," the Prime Minister explained,

> offers social, cultural and definitely political promises. The transformation of the relations of space and time induced by the information networks allows for many democratic hopes, whether it is a matter of access to knowledge and to culture, of regional development, or of the participation of the citizenry in local life.[38]

The majority of the notions about the information society held by the French and European politicians resonate curiously in the ears of those who know a bit about what has already been said on the other side of the Atlantic about these questions since the beginning of the nineties.

An American-inspired theme

In an analysis of these questions,[39] the French researcher Thierry Vedel comments on a great convergence of all these projects at a global level that reveals, he explains, a "common cognitive map." In fact, although the political orientation of the concerned countries differs, they still all agree in giving a central place to that mysterious given: "information," the pivot of the new promise.

Erik Neveu, a French political scientist, in an analysis of the theme of the society of communication, noted, without seeing the religious dimension that this theme contains, that it functions as a "grand narrative," a "coherent structure of

---

[38] Text distributed by the Office of the Prime Minister.
[39] Thierry Vedel, *loc. cit.*

meanings."[40] One of the authors of the "grand narrative," the American Vice-President Al Gore, is the craftsman of a policy aimed at constructing an information society. Under the influence of the Internet fundamentalists, he would make better known the immense promises that this project entailed. He presented his project using quasi-religious accents suitable for seducing the American public, to the point that a convergence of the heritage of the counter-culture with the new, neo-liberal establishment came about in the area of informatics.

The idea of a society reorganized around an information network emerged in November 1991, in the framework of a law proposed by the future vice-president, at that time a senator, entitled "High-Performance Computing Act." That law was followed in 1993 by the announcement of a gigantic project, the National Information Infrastructure project. It became known to the larger public via a speech greatly celebrated by the media, Al Gore's speech before the American Academy of Television Arts and Sciences in Los Angeles on the 11th of January 1994.

The themes of that speech served as the basis and inspiration for the politicians who, throughout the world, henceforth subscribed to the new order of the day: the necessity of submitting society to the new cult of information. What was heard on that day? First that language must be reformed: "The future of language" Gore said,

> is in our hands. Or put more broadly, the future of communications. As we prepare to enter the new millennium, we are learning a new language. It will be the *lingua franca* of the new era. It is made up of ones and zeroes and bits and bytes. But as we master it, as we bring the digital revolution into our homes and schools, we will be able to communicate

---

[40] Erik Neveu, *Une société de communication?* Montchrestien, Paris, 1997, p. 63.

ideas and information... with an ease never before thought possible.[41]

Language, henceforth, must become information.

Playing upon all the registers of the promise, Gore then announced that "our new ways of communication after this revolution will entertain as well as inform. More importantly, they will educate, promote democracy and save lives. And in the process they will also create a lot of new jobs." It would be difficult for a politician to make more extensive claims for the social changes that may be brought about. The future vice-president announced that "the information revolution will change everyone's way of living, working and interacting"! These speeches thus appear to be a curious mixture of typical politics and of promises in which the formulation has religious accents that we must seek to understand better. In any case they laid the foundation for the new "cult of the Internet." A new religiosity is on the move, in which the global information society will be the main showcase. What is the spirit of this new religiosity?

The foundations of the information society

Two American books, widely known not only in America but throughout the world, contributed greatly to establishing the framework of the promise. The first, *Being Digital,* by Nicholas Negroponte, was written in the form of a popular essay.[42] The second was written in another literary genre of which Americans are fond, the didactic autobiography of a man who was "successful in life," and who, "beginning from nothing," became one of the richest men in the world. It fur-

---

[41] Al Gore, "Remarks as delivered by Vice President Al Gore to the Super-highway Summit, Royce Hall, UCLA, Los Angeles, California, January 11, 1994. Available at: http://clinton1.nara.gov/White_House/EOP/OVP/other/superhig.html
[42] Nicholas Negroponte, *Being Digital, op. cit.*

nishes models of behavior and identification, at the same time as it convinces that success is "in your hands" for whoever will make the effort. That is the case of Bill Gates, founder and principal actor of Microsoft, which designs and sells computer software throughout the world.[43]

Nicholas Negroponte is the director of the Medialab at the prestigious Massachussetts Institute of Technology; that great school of engineers has long been associated with technological innovation. Negroponte is also director of the Centre nationale de l'informatique in France. His book is an appeal for us to systematically adopt informatics in every aspect of our lives. "The digital" describes the landscape of a New Jerusalem. The author pleads for the establishment of a truly new world: "The true value of a network is less about information and more about community. The information superhighway ... is creating a totally new global social fabric."[44]

We are also summoned with a promise, since, according to that American researcher,

> Being digital nevertheless does give much cause for optimism. Like a force of nature, the digital age cannot be denied or stopped. It has four very powerful qualities that will result in its ultimate triumph: decentralizing, globalizing, harmonizing and empowering.[45]

If we follow the author on this point, there is nothing to do except to give in to it, and everything will be made better. The cult of the Internet, if it is practiced with meticulous care in all aspects of our lives, as it demands, will change the world.

Bill Gates also has no doubts about the promising character of the new tools. His personal experience argues in all

---

[43] Bill Gates, *The Road Ahead*, Viking, New York, 1995.
[44] Nicholas Negroponte, *Being Digital, op. cit.*, p. 183.
[45] *Ibid.*, p. 229.

cases in favor of its economic virtues. The patron of Micro-soft is at the junction of two American mythologies of which he makes an admirable synthesis. The first is that of the belief in the strongly positive effects of technology. The second is that of the man who begins with nothing and rises through all the levels of society.

In the seventies, Bill Gates was just a young student of technology (which in the Unites States was previously the bottom of the professional ladder) especially taken with the "counter-culture," and close to those who, in their hearts, dreamt of changing the world thanks to a new object, the microcomputer. According to legend, Gates, in his garage, conceived the first software allowing the machines to work, which Steve Jobs, then recently converted to Zen Buddhism, and Steve Wosniak would finish, and which the company Apple was to make known to the world.

Some thirty years later, after many hard-won industrial and commercial battles, and in spite of some recent disap-pointments such as the threat of the dismantling of his enter-prise, the young libertarian had accumulated one of the great-est fortunes in the United States, notably owning twenty per-cent of Microsoft, listed on the stock exchange at the begin-ning of the year 2000 at nothing less than 500 billion dollars (by way of comparison, the annual budget of France is on the order of 300 billion dollars).

To be at the top of a fortune greater than that of the cu-mulative budgets of many Third World nations, or even of that of the French National Defense (nuclear program in-cluded), apparently gives him a certain confidence when speaking on his subject. His work, *The Road Ahead*, is replete with a somewhat naive certainty about what can only be un-derstood as a belief that what happened to him could happen to anyone in the world, at the same time as he has no doubts about his own personal qualities. Translated into French in 1995, this book announced the reign of "total interactivity" and of the "ultimate market." The promise is formulated thus: "There will be a day, not far distant, when you will be able to conduct business, study, explore the world and its cultures, call up any great entertainment, make friends, attend neighborhood markets, and show pictures to distant relatives—without leaving your desk or your armchair." The author continues by announcing "a new, mediated way of life."[46]

After explaining to us at length how the technologies function and especially how they allow us to transform the least of our thoughts and actions into "information," the author concludes that all this is just a beginning:

> I'm optimistic about the impact of the new technology. It will enhance leisure time and enrich culture by expanding the distribution of information. It will help relieve pressures on urban areas by enabling individuals to work from home or remote-site offices. It will relieve pressure on natural resources because increasing numbers of products will be able to take the form of bits rather than manufactured goods. It will give us more control over our lives. [...] Citizens of the information society will enjoy new opportunities for productivity, learning, and entertainment.[47]

There also one finds the point of view regarding technology expressed as a promise of vast import: to remake practically all aspects of our lives.

This promise shines brightest in the works of Pierre Lévy, whose many essays on this theme have had a great influence on the world of the new information technologies and beyond. Set at a very high degree of generality, Lévy does not hesitate to evoke the "global reconnection of the human species with itself"[48] which the Internet will permit. His vision

---

[46] Bill Gates, *The Road Ahead, op. cit.*, p. 4-5.

[47] *Ibid.*, p. 250.

[48] Pierre Lévy, *World philosophie*, op. cit., p. 20.

reverberates on occasion with the anthropological vision of Teilhard de Chardin, where mankind, at first united in the earliest stage of humanity's existence (the first human communities of East Africa), then separated by dispersion over the whole planet (the period of migrations followed by the foundation of the great cities), finally finds itself in a vast "collective consciousness" which will be the profound culmination of the species:

> We shall extend a little the curve of convergence by our involvement through the consideration of what separates us. We have just emerged from prehistory. The separations are the somber part of our heritage, on the way to a progressive liquidation. The true destination of mankind is to be global, actively participating in the collective intelligence of the species.[49]

In this view the Internet represents, to use the author's own phrase, a "citadel of light."

The religious and mystical dimension is explicitly present here, expressing with great precision the more or less latent traits of those who see the Internet as the source of a new promise for mankind and the world. Whether it is a matter of fundamentalists such as Pierre Lévy, Bill Gates and Nicholas Negroponte, or any number of other essayists and politicians, they all fall into step; Americans, Europeans, and Japanese, the theme is the same: a unilaterally optimistic promise with a strong religious tone. It covers a vast territory and concerns most aspects of our social and individual lives. For all these authors it constitutes the true purpose of the new information technologies. Two points insistently recur. The first, in outline but nonetheless systematically present, concerns the question of social violence. Everything proceeds as if the Internet has the power to "reduce tensions," to construct a

---

[49] *Ibid.*, p. 47.

"more harmonious," less antagonistic social bond. The imaginary world that this discourse promises us is calm, luminous and pacified.

The second recurrent theme is that curious model of social relation, presented most often as obvious: the systematic valorization of the "possibility of doing everything alone" without leaving your seat, as Bill Gates says. Thus, Pierre Lévy predicts,

> in the first decades of the 21st century, [...] the greater part of social life will take place in cyberspace, the main environment for communication and for social life. The Internet represents simply that state of humanity's regrouping which will succeed the physical village. One will find almost all of the activities that one finds in the village plus many more, completely new.[50]

Mitchell Kapor, another Internet fundamentalist, described some of the stakes of the new social bond in *Wired* magazine:

> In fact, life in cyberspace seems to be shaping up exactly like Thomas Jefferson would have wanted: founded on the primacy of individual liberty and a commitment to pluralism, diversity, and community. [...] Yet... crucial doubts remain as to whether the re-wiring of America will result in Jeffersonian networks promoting the openness, freedom, and diversity that is the true promise of this technology."[51]

The ideal of life that prepared the new cult of the Internet presents itself right off as fundamentally moral.

What exactly is the nature of the religiosity at work in this new "cult," and that we see in this theme of the global information society? It seems that certain original traits are to be

---

[50] *Ibid.*, p. 57.
[51] Mitchell Kapor, "Where is the digital highway really heading?" *Wired*, issue 1.03, July-August 1993.

found there which are not easily interpreted. Accents reminiscent of Teilhard de Chardin that characterize the language of Pierre Lévy must not hide the fact that his promise of accessing a "reunified universal consciousness" is also nourished by Buddhist sources. The inventor of the computer on which the lines you are reading were composed, Steve Jobs, creator of the Macintosh line of products, was heavily influenced by Zen Buddhism, having previously been a Zen monk. At the same time, we certainly see that we are dealing with new categories, even as ancient themes forcefully present themselves.

Before exploring these paths linked to the counter-culture and Eastern influences, it will be useful to go back a bit to that key moment at the beginning of informatics when some had already imagined that "information" was more than a simple technical fact, and that the future of humanity would take place in the context of a radical revolution towards a "society of global communication." At the origin of all this one finds a *vision*, that of an entirely open and transparent universe—if only opacity, disorder and entropy were not lying in wait for it. That vision was perhaps the point of departure for the whole adventure.

3.

The incarnation of a vision

The enthusiastic discourses concerning the Internet often draw their legitimacy from their newness; their capacity to mobilize the energies of young people hangs on that. Advertising does not fail to associate the new information technologies and above all that which they can do, with the taste of the never-before seen and the rejection of all conformity. That presentation of the facts masks the old age of the theme of the information society.

Curiously, a more thorough investigation turns up an extraordinary constancy of this theme since the 1950s. One might even establish that it is the object of a cyclical "rediscovery." Born in the immediately post-war period, this project of a new society reorganized around communication (reduced to its purely informational dimension) has since known various avatars. From the fifties on, a number of works of science fiction proposed such a society and described with precision the Internet, multimedia, and virtual communication; Isaac Asimov's *Naked Sun* is one such example.[52]

Already in the sixties American essayists like Daniel Bell, Alvin Toffler and Zbigniew Brzezinski spoke of a "third wave" of civilization, coming after agriculture and industry

---

[52] Isaac Asimov. *Naked Sun*, Ballantyne, New York, 1983 (first published in 1956).

and centered on the immaterial.[53] The model of the new society, according to Daniel Bell, is formed by the "charismatic community" of scholars, science forming for these latter a "sacred" quality as the way of life of its members. Bell saw in the new information society an eminently religious dimension:

> Like Christianity, this charismatic dimension has within it a recurrent utopian and even messianic appeal. It is the tension between those charismatic elements and the realities of large-scale organization that will frame the political realities of science in the post-industrial society.[54]

Alvin Toffler evokes how for him, "A powerful tide is surging across much of the world today," and explains that "the human story, far from ending, has only just begun."[55] Zbigniew Brzezinski invented and for a while popularized the expression "technetronic era."

Very early on (1962), McLuhan popularized his "global village" which would appear thanks to the "electronic media." His influence should not be underestimated. For Mattelart, all the essayists of the information society are positioned in relationship to that professor from Toronto who "reconstructed a religious vision of global integration applicable to every stage of the information age."[56] The current director of the McLuhan program at the University of Toronto confirmed that the religious faith of McLuhan, who converted as an adult to Catholicism, had inspired his thought.

---

[53] See the analysis of Armand Mattelart in "L'âge de l'information. Genèse d'une appellation non contrôlée," *Réseaux*, no 101, Hermès Science Publications, Paris, 2000.

[54] Daniel Bell, *The Coming of Post-Industrial Society. A Venture in Social Forecasting*, Basic Books, New York, 1973, p. 408.

[55] Alvin Toffler, *The Third Wave*, Morror, New York, 1980.

[56] Armand Mattelart, *The Information Society: An Introduction*, Sage, London, 2001, p. 68

In fact, a reading of his famous work *The Gutenberg Galaxy* makes clear the singular influence of the Jesuit father Teilhard de Chardin, the inventor of the notion of the "noosphere," which is for the intellect what the "biosphere is for life,"[57] and which McLuhan interprets as "the technological brain for the world," "the cosmic membrane that has been snapped round the globe by the electric dilation of our various senses."[58] This religious global vision attempts a synthesis of the sciences and religion. That was the theme, well fitting the spirit of the age, of a large UNESCO colloquium in 1965, in memory of both Einstein and Teilhard de Chardin.[59] It was also one of the hopes of another plan marked by Eastern philosophy and parapsychology, the review *Planète*, co-founded by Jacques Bergier and Louis Pauwels, which had its moment of glory in the sixties.

In order to understand in depth the discourse surrounding the information society, the promises that it carries and the religiosity in which it is bathed, it is necessary to press the enquiry all the way to the source. Thus one may be able to better perceive the reasons for its growing success and its deepest nature. The only real difference between the discourse on the information society of yesterday and that of today is that it has left the circle of specialists who gave it birth and now reaches a vast public. The cult of information has been realized and popularised *via* the cult of the Internet.

An old story

The root "cyber" joined to all sorts of words indicates the starting point. We should not forget, Armand Mattelart re-

---

[57] Pierre Teilhard de Chardin, *Le phénomène humain*, Seuil, Paris, 1955. English edition: *The Phenomenon of Man*, Harper, New York, 1959.

[58] Marshall McLuhan, *The Gutenberg Galaxy: The Making of Typographic Man*, University of Toronto, Toronto, 1962, p. 32.

[59] *Science et synthèse*, Gallimard/Unesco, Paris, 1967.

minds us,[60] that it was in the heart of "cybernetics," invented by the American mathematician Norbert Wiener[61] in the 1940s, that what could be called the first "cult of information" was born. Wiener, and following him numerous cyberneticists who spread the "good news," in effect defended a fuller vision of the world which makes "information" (in the larger sense, not just mediated information) the hard core of a global representation of the real. A genuine paradigm gradually developed out of this research, of which we shall give an account here.

That "informational" vision of the world forms the basis and background of current discussions of the Internet and the Information Society. It is this vision that gives the discourse its diffuse religiosity. The expansion of this paradigm continued throughout the half century that followed, touching more and more numerous and diversified areas, such as automation, informatics and artificial intelligence, biology and genetics, humanities and social sciences (where it was implicit from the beginning), philosophy and psychoanalysis, communication sciences and the media, and the field of political ideas. Today that vision has crystallized around the Internet.

Along the way, this theme has combined with other currents of thought which, especially in the nineteenth century, evoked, in their own ways, a "new society." Armand Mattelart put together evidence of the links between the contemporary ideology of communication and the very old theme of the "global utopia,"[62] while Pierre Musso precisely described the influence of the Saint-Simonian notion of networks on

---

[60] Armand Mattelart, *Histoire de l'utopie planétaire, op. cit.*, especially p. 311.

[61] For a more detailed presentation of these ideas of Norbert Wiener, see: Philippe Breton, *L'utopie de la communication, op. cit.*; Steve J. Heims, *John Von Neumann and Norbert Wiener*, MIT Press, Cambridge, Mass., 1982; and Jean-Pierre Dupuy, *Aux origines des sciences cognitives*, La Découverte, Paris, 1992.

[62] Armand Mattelart, *Histoire de l'utopie planétaire, op. cit.*

current discussions of the Internet.[63] However, it was Wiener and his cybernetics who laid the foundations for the "cult of information" and the march of proselytes that accompanied the new paradigm. Norbert Wiener was at the origin of a new "vision of the world," rather radical in the rupture which it proposed.

Information according to Wiener

We can summarize Wiener's approach in the following manner: the world—and therefore all beings dependent upon it, whatever they may be—is composed of two great elements. There are forms, ideas, messages, "information" (all these terms are equivalent here), and there is disorder, chance, and entropy. On the one hand, spirit; on the other, matter. Information is thus defined, in a manner both extraordinarily general and reductive at the same time, as the "name for the content of what is exchanged with the outer world as we adjust to it, and make our adjustment felt upon it."[64]

Entropy, the negation of information, is not a simple theoretical fact. According to Wiener (who explicitly employs theological developments on this matter), its actual presence in the universe is comparable to imperfection, chance, disorder, disorganization, or death. Entropy represents a fundamental violence against which information alone allows one to fight. In the end, Wiener associates it with the "Devil," while remaining within the framework of atheist thought. We shall return later on to these apparent contradictions upon which the cult of information is based.

---

[63] Pierre Musso, *Télécommunications et philosophie des réseaux. La postérité paradoxale de Saint-Simon, op. cit.*
[64] Norbert Wiener, *The Human Use of Human Beings: Cybernetics and Society*, 2nd ed. rev., Doubleday Anchor, New York, 1956, p. 17.

Entropy and information are therefore the two faces of one same reality, of *the* reality. Whatever has value in the world is on the side of information. In this sense, everything (except the occurrence of entropic crimes) is information, message, movement. All being is, essentially, in its deepest existence, message. This thought inaugurated what one may call a "radical ontology of the message": nothing exists except in the form of a message, information, a potential transparence. We are brought to a true mystique of communication. The finality of the message is circular; everything that goes along with the movement is positive; everything that conspires in restraining the movement of information is its opposite: entropy, disorder, Evil.

The new vision of the world defended by Wiener is presented—without directly formulating it thus—as an "anti-metaphysical" approach, in that it postulates that there is nothing whatsoever behind the real, reducing it to the continual and visible exchange of the information which constitutes it. It is important to note that in this conception the reality of objects and natural phenomena is entirely exhausted in the information which constitutes them and which is exchanged in a constant flow. The new paradigm is an idea of relation that encloses the real within the relational, and the relational within the informational.

A new vision of the human being and of society

From these foundations, and with the institutional support of cybernetics, Wiener goes on to explore two major axes of reflection that make up the two central branches of the new information vision of the world. On the one hand, a reflection on the nature of the human which leads him to take up anti-humanist theoretical positions; and on the other, a quasi-sociological reflection on the ideal society which would be built around information.

The information paradigm then immediately gives birth to the project of a "New Man" living in a "new society," the "global information society." Wiener opens the way to the cult of everything-that-favors-the-circulation-of-information. Wiener thus affirms that the human being, according to a fundamental ontological plan, ought to be considered as essentially made up of "information," and from that draws radical conclusions with very contemporary accents.

> The physical identity of an individual does not consist in the matter of which it is made. [...] Since this is so, there is no absolute distinction between the types of transmission which we can use for sending a telegram from country to country and the types of transmission which at least are theoretically possible for transmitting a living organism such as a human being.[65]

And,

> Consider what would happen if we were to transmit the whole pattern of the human body, with its memories and cross connections, so that a hypothetical receiving instrument could re-embody these messages in appropriate matter, capable of continuing the processes already in the body and the mind.[66]

Anticipating certain remarks that would be made about the Internet and cyberspace, Wiener adds that "the fact that we cannot telegraph the pattern of a man from one place to another is probably due to technical difficulties, ... It is not due to any impossibility of the idea."[67]

This new vision was also applied to society in the sense that, for Wiener, "the nature of social communities depends

---

[65] *Ibid.*, p. 101, 103.

[66] *Ibid.*, p. 96.

[67] Norbert Wiener, *The Human Use of Human Beings: Cybernetics and Society*, Houghton Mifflin Co., Boston, 1950, p. 110.

to a large extent upon their intrinsic modes of communication."[68] It follows that

> Society can only be understood through a study of the messages and the communication facilities that belong to it; in the future development of these messages and communication facilities, messages between man and machines, between machines and man, and between machine and machine, are destined to play an ever-increasing part.[69]

The use of the word "only" clearly illustrates that, for him, it is the messages that contain society and what is vital to it. Just as man is defined in terms of information, society is also entirely information. Each man is no longer the center of a world. In this perspective, when "the integrity of the channels of internal communication is essential to the welfare of society,"[70] then "communication is the cement of the society."[71]

The model of society that he designs, in which the central point is information and its circulation, is a society without a State, founded upon small communities of life and on a global communication system. It is a society where the notion of equality is understood, as we have seen, to apply well beyond the realm of the human, since it includes intelligent machines, considering them as potentially the equals of human beings.

Fifty years later, Pierre Lévy, the most recent direct heir of this idea of forms in movement, writes at length about this question, which for him is essential:

> By being interconnected, [...] humanity constitutes itself more and more in the noosphere, in the world of ideas, becoming an active receptacle of forms. This done, the real

---

[68] *Ibid.*, p. 59.
[69] Norbert Wiener, *The Human Use of Human Beings*, 2nd ed. rev., op. cit., p. 16.
[70] *Ibid.*, p. 131.
[71] Norbert Wiener, *The Human Use of Human Beings*, 1950, op. cit., p. 144.

world is discovered to be a world of ideas, a universe of forms.[72]

The author goes on to say that "the history of the universe is precisely that of an acceleration of the production of forms."[73]

Before looking at how these technical devices are going to realize this vision it is necessary to render unto Caesar what is Caesar's: after having created it, Wiener was the first to critique cybernetics and what it became in his eyes. Had he not understood the profoundly anti-humanist import of that new vision of the world? Did he suddenly feel himself to be akin to the sorcerer's apprentice, having "let the genie out of the bottle," without knowing how to put it back? Was he reminded that according to the traditions of the creators of the golem with whom he was connected (he claimed to be a descendent of Rabbi Loew, creator of the Golem of Prague), pious men immediately un-made their creature the same day they brought it into being? However that may be, Wiener would never become a member of the club which he had created. That he separated himself from his vision did not prevent him from being its first prophet.

Norbert Wiener is, partly in spite of himself, at the origin of a current of thought of which the novelty and strangeness of certain aspects no one of the age could escape. It is the intense valorization of information and of communication that came to be the matrix of the new cult. Today, this cult has taken for its object the Internet, but one can see better now that beyond the network itself, it is a matter of more than a simple realization; it is truly another, larger, reality.

The cybernetics that he had created subsequently came to have an extraordinary influence. This can be measured simply by the enormous success of information and of communica-

---

[72] Pierre Lévy, *World philosophie, op. cit.*, p. 211.

[73] *Ibid.*, p. 215.

tion as new ways of regarding the world. These new categories are not simply conceptual tools that are added to others.
The phenomena linked to communication are soon presented
as what it is necessary to observe in order to understand the
world, since the latter is, in its own essence, communication.
Norbert Wiener is at the origin of a *vision* that makes one see
the world differently if one agrees to share it.

Form and information being the same, this new vision of
the world establishes information as the key value, the recog-
nition of which gives direction to progress. This valorization
verges on the sacred. It is in that direction, in the direction of
that vision, that some claim for themselves the mission of
facilitating communication wherever that is possible. In fact,
this means constructing the technical means for which the
primary end will be to permit communication.

Putting the first networks in place

We have seen that the promise of a new society is accompanied by two conditions which were clearly formulated by
Wiener: on the one hand society would be reorganized
around all the technologies that serve to deal with, conserve
and transport information; on the other, everything that can
be put into the form of information must be. In this binary
conception of the world, everything that is neither information nor susceptible of becoming such, is rejected. Yet the
technologies necessary for the fulfillment of that promise did
not yet exist. At the moment in which the new project of society took shape, those technologies still existed only as ideas
or rough sketches.

From the moment that a new device is invented it is immediately hailed as an indispensable stage in the realization of
the new world. In June 1945, John von Neumann, one of the
participants in the seminar that produced cybernetics,
sketched the plans for a new machine capable of imitating

and reproducing the characteristics of the human brain. He thus invented the prototype of the modern computer. Right from the start, the new machine was conceived to be basically a representation of the human brain, which was itself imagined along the lines of the communication of its component parts.[74] We have tried to demonstrate, in an earlier work,[75] that the project of the computer continued a long history of making "artificial creatures," while using a new vision of the human being in which information played a central role.

After the construction of the first computer in England, a discussion began in France and the United States, starting with an article published the 28th of December 1948 in the journal *Le Monde*, by someone who much later would be the advocate for Galileo in the case under review by the Vatican: the Dominican father Dominique Dubarle, a physician well acquainted with Wiener's thought. (The latter commented on his article in a later edition of *The Human Use of Human Beings: Cybernetics and Society*). This text was entitled "Vers la machine à gouverner. Une nouvelle science: la cybernétique" [Towards a machine to govern: a new science, cybernetics].

In that article Dubarle described the computer as a machine destined to be greatly expanded, a machine that would function on a world-wide scale and be quite analogous to the human brain. The informatics literature that followed took up this theme of the unique computer, of a center of universal calculation where a single "brain" would take charge of all problems. The imaginary reference is indeed a single powerful machine, endowed with memory sufficient to surpass the "threshold" that Von Neumann had proposed, beyond which the computer would possess "intelligence."

---

[74] Philippe Breton, "Le premier ordinateur copiait le cerveau humain," *La Recherche*, no 290, septembre 1996.

[75] Philippe Breton, *À l'image de l'homme. Du golem aux créatures virtuelles*, Seuil, Paris, 1996.

Dubarle discussed with precision the applications that would constitute the "rational conduct of human processes," a possibility that leads directly to the new machines having the capacity to "execute the tasks of thinking." The central argument was the following: politicians, and more generally political systems, are incapable of taking charge of the administration of societies on a global scale. The great interest of the new machines is that they permit us to foresee the possibility of a machine that would govern rationally, which would eventually lead to global unification, toward "one government for the planet." We find there the premises of the current debates on the fate of the Internet. In one sense the great questions of this latter debate were already contained in those texts that were written in the last years of the forties and of which Dubarle's article is a good synthesis. A discussion originally limited to certain specialists, the promise of a better world thanks to information and to new information technologies would come to be increasingly widespread.

The influence of cybernetics

From the end of the fifties, in the United States as in Europe, research on cybernetics, the main branch of the information paradigm, really took off. It is difficult now, for various reasons, to give an account of the extent of the science's impact. Its march across the disciplines reached all the sciences, theoretical and applied. It was even the object of a vast campaign of popularization directed at the general public. Cybernetics carried a new vision of the world, global and promising. It proposed a kind of original synthesis between science and a new religiosity.

It was in the same era that Teilhard de Chardin also proposed his original synthesis between science and religion (it appears that father Dubarle had been one of his original Parisian readers): he imagined that the "biosphere," the unity of all the living systems on Earth, would be succeeded by the "noosphere," that collectivism of ideas straining toward a single point.

One of the principal supports of cybernetics would be the notion of the artificial brain, of electronic animals,[76] and later of artificial intelligence. This theme served to promote an informational vision of the human being. It was also in that period that through the popularization campaigns the language of futurism was developed. In this discourse the society of the future was described as being entirely structured by the new technical devices.

During this time the virtues of cybernetics were discovered in the Soviet Union, after having been labeled "bourgeois science" under Stalin. Cybernetics appeared there also as a means for the rational administration of socialist society and as one of the tools for the passage to communism, that is to say, the society without a state of which Marx dreamed. Cybernetics was the ideal means to "paradise on earth," the dream of many communists.

Wiener's lectures in the Soviet Union were undoubtedly related to the diffusion of cybernetic ideas on the other side of the iron curtain. The later implosion of the Soviet system interrupted that experience. In France, these hopes fueled planning efforts that resulted here and there in public enterprises such as RATP [Autonomous Operator of Parisian Transports], for example, in "cybernetic management," lofty sites for imagining a new, more radiant world. Thus one dreamt, like Jacques Bureau, of the coming of a "logical era": "The abolition of the chief, of authority, of dogma and of parties [will permit the arrival] of self-adapting, self-evolving mechanisms."[77]

---

[76] Philippe Breton, "L'oubli de la tortue," *Alliages*, 1991.
[77] Jacques Bureau, *L'ère logique*, Robert Laffont, Paris, 1969, p. 11.

That first period was brought to an end, rather brutally, by a temporary oversight of cybernetics, a "clandestinity," as Abraham Moles would call it. There were many reasons for what happened. So many promises had been made but not fulfilled: an artificial intelligence comparable to human intelligence in "not less than ten years" had been predicted in 1951. Also, too many adventurers had slipped between the interdisciplinary cracks and ruined the reputation of the field. Finally, the strong tendency to specialization in the sciences came up against the project to reunite the sciences under the aegis of the single concept of information. The separation and independent development of informatics in relation to cybernetics led to a provisionally more pragmatic approach.

One could also make the hypothesis that the extremely violent anti-humanist discourse of cybernetics had temporarily irritated and aroused the resistance of certain groups. The religiosity that the movement carried also irritated many scientists. Cybernetics was temporarily caught between two fires.

Many intellectuals were, moreover, explicitly campaigning against cybernetics for a variety of reasons. Jacques Ellul wrote in France and was an important voice in the United States (since 1947); the French philosopher Henri Lefebvre wrote a very critical work on "cybernanthropy" in 1967[78] (The events of '68 also began in Strasbourg with the situationist student protest against the courses of the French cyberneticist Abraham Moles); and the German philosopher Jürgen Habermas sharply criticized cybernetics for its central role in the bringing about of "science and technology as ideology."[79]

---

[78] Henri Lefebvre, *Position: contre les technocrates*, Méditations, Paris, 1967 (le titre de la première édition était *Le cybernanthrope*).

[79] Jürgen Habermas, *Technik und Wissenschaft als "Ideologie,"* Suhrkamp, 1968.

In the sixties, the old cybernetic discourse was again reha-bilitated. This time, it was not simply the concern of engi-neers or mathematicians. The notion of information set in motion by Wiener had jumped the boundaries of that world and spread through the human sciences. In Europe a certain number of researchers were susceptible to the siren's song of the information paradigm. That was the case with Jacques Lacan, whose new conception of the unconscious undoubt-edly owed much to cybernetics, including themes he had dis-cussed since 1954; or Claude Lévi-Strauss, who still today insists upon a vision of the world in which entropy occupies an important place; or, even more, Edgar Morin, in whose thought the cybernetic origin is explicit. In the field of phi-losophy, we note, among others, Jean-François Lyotard, who, in 1979, attempted a synthesis of post-modernism[80] that ap-pealed largely to the fundamental concepts of the information paradigm.

The history of the influence of the information paradigm in the humanities and social sciences has just begun to be written.[81] Undoubtedly many surprises will be found, as well as the keys to certain debates that were wrongly believed to be intellectually new. The influence of cybernetics and of the information paradigm in biology is equally strong: the notion of information conceptually nourished the discovery of the genetic code at the beginning of the 1950s. A whole concep-tual lexicon was imported, even the notion of "program."

---

[80] Jean-François Lyotard, *La Condition Postmoderne*, Minuit, Paris, 1979. Eng-lish translation: *The Postmodern Condition: a Report on Knowledge*, University of Minnesota, Minneapolis, 1984.

[81] As an example: Céline Lafontaine, *Cybernétique et sciences humaines: aux origines d'une représentation informationnelle du sujet,* Université de Montréal, 2001.

The "double helix" is indeed an information-centric view carried all the way into the heart of the living.[82]

The immense field opened up by genetic manipulation found its principal underpinning in the cybernetic idea of the new man, who could be detached from his initial nature to be remodeled at will. Genetics in this sense is nothing other than the capture of the "model of the human being," which one can then put into circulation in the communication network to be enhanced, civilized, and as the German philosopher Peter Sloterdijk, direct heir of cybernetics, would later say, "domesticated."[83] Yet it was within the field of informatics and the new information technologies that the idea of a society better reorganized around communication routes found itself taking shape. This new vision of the world nourished the world of the computer programmers, who in turn became its principal missionaries. The religiosity that accompanied the first cybernetics would finally be realized.

Microcomputers and the origins of the Internet

The beginning of the eighties saw the origins of the Internet, which went from being an application connected with the military—ARPANet—to a group of large public networks, a transition well described in Jean-Claude Guédon's work on the subject.[84] (See also the work of Christian Huitema *Et Dieu créa Internet* [*And God created the Internet*][85]). "Cyber" became a widely used prefix.

---

[82] Michel Morange, *Histoire de la biologie moléculaire*, La Découverte, Paris, 1994.

[83] Sloterdijk thus situates himself in the camp of "cyber-biotechnics" and argues in favor of the replacement of "metaphysical discontinuities by postmetaphysical continuities" (Peter Sloterdijk, "Le centrisme mou au risque de penser," *Le Monde*, 9 October, 1999).

[84] Jean-Claude Guédon, *La planète cyber. Internet et le cyberespace*, Gallimard, coll. "Découvertes," Paris, 1996.

[85] Christian Huitema, *Et Dieu créa Internet*, Eyrolles, Paris, 1996.

From the beginning the world of the networks was closely associated with that promise of another form of communication, or rather of a universe where communication would have the whole place, the central place. The French researcher Patrice Flichy, specialist in the history of communication technologies, documented the discourse of the founders of the new communications networks that were the matrix of the Internet. He refers to the "republic of the programmers."[86] Other networks had existed earlier, but they were technically very limited by design, such as the network SAGE, put in place in the 1950's by the United States Army in order to prepare for an eventual Soviet threat.

The great difference with the new networks is that these latter were born "spontaneously" in the American informatics scene, as a tool for internal work and at the same time as a support for a new social relationship carrying numerous promises. From that it follows that this would concern not only the world of informatics but the world as a whole. Patrice Flichy demonstrated how certain "ARPAnauts" had a clear understanding of their mission, as many texts written in the seventies testify: "We in the ARPA community (and no doubt many others outside it) have come to realize that we have in our hands something very big, and possibly very important. It is now plain to all of us that messenger service over computer networks has enormous potential for changing the way communication is done in all sectors of our society, military, civilian government, and private."[87]

Thirty years later, echoing these promises, Pierre Lévy analyzed that history thus:

---

[86] Patrice Flichy, "Internet ou la communauté scientifique idéale," *Réseaux*, no 97, CNET/Hermès Science Publications, 1999.
[87] Cited in Patrice Flichy, *loc. cit.*, p. 92. [English version taken from P. Flichy, *The Internet Imaginaire*, MIT Press, 2007, p. 47]

By offering the Internet to the world, the scientific community made a gift of the technical infrastructure of a collective
intelligence which is without doubt its finest discovery. It
has also transmitted to the rest of humanity its best invention, that of its own mode of sociability, of its human type,
and of its communication.[88]

As early as 1968, the two celebrated precursors of the Internet, American researchers Licklider and Taylor (this latter
being responsible for the information department of ARPA)
clearly affirmed that, "In a few years, men will be able to
communicate more effectively through a machine than face
to face. That is a rather startling thing to say, but it is our
conclusion."[89]

In 1978 an American work with the evocative title, *The
Network Nation: Human Communication Via Computer,* written
by Murray Turoff and Starr Hiltz, sketched a tableau of the
future to which we are now habituated:

When such systems become widespread, potentially intense
communication networks among geographically dispersed
persons will become actualized. We will become the Network Nation, exchanging vast amounts of both information
and social-emotional communications...[90]

As early as 1976 the term "collective intelligence" was used in
this context.

The ambience of that era profoundly marked the personality of all those who participated in the adventure of the new
technologies. Thus, Steve Jobs, creator of Apple, Inc. and of

---

[88] Pierre Lévy, *World philosophie, op. cit.,* p. 90.

[89] Cited in Patrice Flichy, *loc. cit.,* p. 97. [English version taken from the
original paper: The computer as a communication device, by J.C.R. Licklider and Robert W. Taylor, *Science and Technology,* April 1968, p. 21]

[90] Cited in Patrice Flichy, *ibid.,* p. 95. [English version taken from: Starr
Roxanne Hiltz and Murray Turoff, *The Network Nation: Human Communication via Computer,* MIT Press, revised edition, 1993, p. xxv]

the Macintosh computer, had stirred up a particular spirit in his company and beyond among the users of microcomputers. After having recalled the different stages of the spiritual life of Mr. Jobs (initiation voyage to India, follower of the "New Age," then conversion to Zen Buddhism in 1975), one of his biographers narrates how he demanded of his employees that they…

> …had to fit the Apple mold; … they had to be believers. Steve's evangelism and belief in the goodness of the dream, the truth of computers, took hold and spread throughout the employee base. People came to Apple who had found the religion, and they in turn pushed the religion further. It was evangelical fervor, a sect that grew from Cupertino and blazed across the country. If you didn't catch the religion, or tried to buck the system, you were excommunicated.[91]

With the development of microcomputers, and after the number of computers had increased sufficiently, the material base was laid for a vast network that would permit their interconnection. In fact, the Internet would rapidly emerge into daily life, interfering each day a bit more in our daily life and acquiring that popularity which we now know. Besides its function as a tool—which, we must not forget, constitutes one of the reasons for its development—it served as a support for the new fundamentalists who saw in the new technologies the incarnation of a vision of the world where form would be everything. The cult of the Internet went on to support a universe of belief that we shall endeavor to understand better, before looking at its limits and dangers.

---

[91] Jeffrey S. Young. *Steve Jobs: the Journey is the Reward.* Scott, Foresman & Co., Glenview IL and London, 1988, p. 160.

4.

A universe of belief

The cult of the Internet is based on a number of beliefs, often strongly reductive since they all lead back to a single factor. The point of departure and the center from which these beliefs radiate is the vision of the world in which the sole reality, the sole truth, is information. The term "information" is of an extraordinary plasticity.[92] For those who employ it in this context it is the equivalent of message, of communication, of form or model. To see information behind the appearance of things and beings: this is to see reality; to exalt information: that is to extract the truth. Reality and truth are mixed; we are indeed within the realm of belief. Information is at the same time what one uses concretely when communicating and the ultimate goal to be attained.

As we have seen, the new religiosity looks toward the construction of a new society, to the putting in place of a new social bond, in which the end will be some kind of cult dedicated to communication. The global information society may be defined as a world thus "transparent to itself," a world that would finally make violence withdraw and which would constitute the ultimate ideal of civilization. The notion of "trans-

---

[92] For a lengthy discussion of this very point see Uwe Pörksen, *Plastic words*, Pennsylvania State University, University Park, 1995.-tr.

parence" is essential. It is indeed around this that the new religiosity, which we shall try to characterize here, is articulated.

An ideal of transparence

The ideal of transparence constitutes the cosmological vision of the new cult, that toward which it tends, the object of the promise, the New Jerusalem toward which the "globalists" aspire. This notion of transparence is consubstantial with the cult of information. It has both practical and spiritual implications: it conditions the concrete activity of those who use the technologies at the same time as it constitutes the ideal of a luminous world, without sin, without entropy. Transparence is, in the heart of this new mystique, a state which one tries to attain. Transparence refers to an ideal of light, harmony, and ecstasy. It gives the impression of "passing through to the other side of the mirror."

Solar metaphors

Pierre Lévy, like many authors in this milieu, multiplies metaphors that are all attached to that ideal: "light," "clarity," "openness." Evoking the search for the "impersonal light" that permits the collective consciousness, he asks: "What is the direction of all this movement? Where is evolution going? What do the 'globalists' want? Note well the speed of the process: the growing interconnection and unification of humanity accompanies the opening of all dimensions."[93] Philippe Quéau both uses and abuses metaphors that link the new world to light when, for example, he evokes the universe of cyberspace as "of Babylons not in confusion, of gardens hanging from lips and fingers, of labyrinths hidden in every point of themselves, in an immense complexity while trans-

---

[93] Pierre Lévy, *World philosophie*, op. cit., p. 21.

parent, easy of access, crystalline, without ceasing to be dense, developed, unceasingly revealing themselves."[94]

The cult of transparence that sees the absolute ideal in a completely open world approaches that evolution of humanity which Teilhard de Chardin looked toward and which he tried to express through the notions of "*diaphanie*," of "transparent bubble," of "milky clarity" and of "translucent flesh." In general, what Jean-Jacques Wunenburger calls the "solar rhetoric of the look and of transparence"[95] is present in all the great religions. The descriptions of the "Heavenly Jerusalem" in different mystical currents—Jewish, Christian and Muslim—appealed in large part to these metaphors of light and of transparence: "The city of celestial light, a place endowed with immaterial corporeality, the Heavenly Jerusalem could only be described through the eyes of the soul."[96] Certain visions of cyberspace do not depart from such a framework.

The search for ecstasy

The influence of certain New Age practices, notably hallucinogenic drugs, is not always a stranger to this belief in transparence. This is how the biographer of Steve Jobs narrates the intellectual process of the invention of the Macintosh:

> For Steve and the other Apple acid-heads, the PARC experience [it had to do with research and development at Xerox] was like dropping acid for the first time and getting the big insight—*satori* [a state of mystical ecstasy]. This was the *tao* of high technology, the right way to build a com-

---

[94] Philippe Quéau, *Le virtuel, virtues et vertiges*, Champ-Vallon, Seysel, 1993, p. 43.
[95] Jean-Jacques Wunenburger, "Regard et transparence, utopie et philosophie," *Quaderni*, no 40, Éditions Sapientia, Paris, 1999-2000, p. 153.
[96] Ibid., p. 153.

puter. With LSD they had seen the layers peel away, felt the very essence of the beingness of a flower or dived into a piece of wood. [...] Like opening the doors of perception, this was crossing the boundary. It was the electronic acid test. If you got the idea, you were on the bus. If you didn't, you were left at the curb.[97]

Ecstasy, *"satori,"* is here clearly associated with the search for transparence that lets one see the reality of things in their "information skeleton." It is to see the real, that is, to see the model of the real hidden behind the materiality of things. The moment of that perception is often seen as a "sacred" time. Many testimonies make clear two constants: one, the sensation of a contraction of time that people say they experience when they are on the network; the other, the feeling that during that time they have reached a vast world apart, sometimes described as the "vast world beneath things." Time passed in front of the machine has nothing to do with ordinary time. It is the time of access to the cosmos. The "bubble effect," which consists in feeling oneself isolated from the world, absorbed in play, is accompanied by a subjective experience of the passage of time which is always that time passes much more quickly in these situations.

The other side of the mirror

In such a spirit—and this is not using the Internet as a simple tool for communication—the actual practice on the network passes into a universe of rules that refer everything to the search for the transparence of the world. The information procedures that one must use refer to a world of order, a world where one puts "the order into things." That quest is in the realm of the mystical and can produce the curious sensation that one has access to the fundamental rules that orga-

---

[97] Jeffrey S. Young. *Steve Jobs*, op. cit., p. 174-175.

nize *everything*. In a world conceived as a permanent struggle between order and disorder (and the place where most mortals live is both that which is made and that which is unmade) the new mystics have the noteworthy privilege of being those through whom order arrives.

The spirit of logic, the sense of organization, and the search for transparence are not only mental qualities, but each is also a mode of being in the world, as well as a means of transforming it. As the laws of organization are supposed to be the same everywhere, the simple fact of having access to a small part of the architecture of the ordered universe in the form of the computer and the network permits one to enter into symbiosis with the whole cosmos, at least with its luminous aspect.

The network is, then, a point of passage for reaching the other side of the mirror. We know that the apparent naiveté of Alice's voyage "to Wonderland" was a means for the author Lewis Carroll (who was previously a logician), to initiate children to the rules of the universe of logic. Wonderland is a world of order and disorder, and the impertinent questions of Alice make up a clear line of demarcation between that which lies on the one side—informational logic—and what lies on the other: Evil, embodied by disorder, chance, the lack of coherence due to disregard of the elementary laws of logic. The quest for transparence truly permits the passage to the other side of the mirror, to see the "being of things."

The quest for harmony

The utopia of the city of glass is often that of a harmonious world, with neither secrets nor lies, neither opposition nor conflict. The notion of transparence, as Gilles Lapouge reminds us,[98] is also an old value belonging to the family of

---

[98] Gilles Lapouge, *Utopie et civilisations*, Albin Michel, Paris, 1990.

utopian ideas. In that sense, it renews an old belief that wanted social harmony to be dependent on the external display of all human behavior in an ideal "city of glass." The Italian philosopher Gianni Vattimo remarks on this subject,

> The society of unrestricted communication in which the community of logical socialism is realized is a transparent society. It manages radically to reduce motives for conflict, precisely by eliminating obstacles and opacity.[99]

To change the world thanks to the Internet, to render it more harmonious, implies the renunciation of conflict, of oppositions, of criticism, of the games of power. Pierre Lévy thus argues at length for the necessity of an "undivided consciousness" concretely embodying (so to speak) that historic vision of the striving towards transparence, that "City of Light," the New Jerusalem of the Internet.

The value of exclusion

In the world of the new information technologies, the theme of "transparence" frequently returns under forms more or less vulgarized. Transparence is at work from the beginning: computers, then the networks, the new magic wands, are supposed to make transparent whatever they touch. One often hears it said, for example, that informatics and now the networks are capable of "making governance transparent." For a long time the same thing has been said in reference to business. The Internet thus presents itself as a tool enabling the struggle against "opacity," the key anti-value of that universe.

That value has also erupted in the world of politics. The Prime Minister of France, Lionel Jospin, at the inauguration of the 19th Summer University of Communications on the

---

[99] Gianni Vattimo, *The Transparent Society*. Johns Hopkins University Press, Baltimore, 1992, p. 20.

25th of August 1998 declared that "the entry of our country into the information society" corresponded to "more access to knowledge and culture, more employment and growth, more public service and transparence, more democracy and liberty." Here transparency is put on the same level as these other values judged to be fundamental.

Transparence is an ideal that serves to exalt, but also, above all, to exclude: what is transparent is, by nature, more evolved, more advanced. "Power," because it is assumed to be the retention of information, is on the side of the dark and the old. "Cooperation," a notion even much more abstract, is on the side of light. "Start-ups" are presented as models of non-hierarchical societies where everything is transparent in every respect. On the side of power, law is more and more presented as an obstacle to putting in place a global information society. In cyberspace, one hears repeated in unison that there is no need for law, least of all national or international laws.

In order to carry out their mission, which is to support the light, information systems themselves must be transparent. From this perspective, all desire to separate systems, to protect them from "external intrusion," is therefore considered antinomian. A good system should be open, transparent. The new religiosity is profoundly antagonistic to the constraints and necessities of what the professionals call "information security," which is simply a variation of the security of goods and persons.

As one can see from some of the examples cited, the pursuit of an ideal of transparence implies the negative requalification of everything which is secret, of the hidden, the private, the intimate, the profound, the non-visible. The actual annihilation of the "non-visible," deemed opaque, cannot help but be an attack on barriers, frontiers, on all separations which impede the flow of information, the "generalized interconnection" and the final transparence of the world.

Many of these barriers would be particularly valuable to target and become the object of a will to subversion, as for example, to take the most important of these, that which separates public from private life, law and juridical norms, all the norms which would impede the "free circulation" of information on the network, and finally, last but not least, the embodiment of speech as an obstacle to free communication.

The ideal of transparence above all takes the form of a war against opacity and obscurity. The new religiosity takes us into a new era through a binary vision of the world. On the one side, information, openness, light; on the other, closure, entropy, disorder, Evil. In one case, a "solar" mode (the planet described by Asimov was aptly named "Solaria"), in the other, shadows.

The struggle against shadows is a real fight, step by step, even if the participants do not always discern the scope and the stakes of the battle. Some are often more concerned with the abolition of the "insupportable frontiers" between the private and the public, others more motivated by the desire to make a leap over all the barriers to access to different parts of the great information network, while, finally, still others are particularly indignant at the restraints to the free circulation of ideas in the form of national laws, the institution of the rights of the author, or, in another area, the presence of numerous middle-men (teachers, businesspeople, journalists) who "interpose" themselves between producers and consumers.

To each one his battle, but all concur in the openness and transparence which are the final truths of the cult of the Internet. In the remaining sections of this chapter we will examine successively four of these "dark spots" whose effacement is the object of all the prayers of the fundamentalists, and which we shall see concern all essential aspects of the social bond: private life, the Law, mediation and embodied speech.

The ideal of openness, or the rejection of the distinction between private and public life

A certain number of particularly devout and militant internauts devote themselves to demonstrating the advantages to be had, according to them, in dissolving the "traditional" barrier between private and public life. Only the pursuit of that very abstract ideal of transparence could explain actions so "out of line" in comparison to our usual behavior as those which consist, for example, in using the Internet to show "to the whole world" their modest private life. Recently, the world is full of experiences of that type. The newspaper *Le monde* devoted two full pages to Yves Eudes' account of an experiment of this type conducted in Ohio.[100]

The reporter describes the affair thus:

> The large blue house is no ordinary place [...] Everything that happens may be seen and heard throughout the planet. Erik, the initiator of the project Here & Now, and his five friends live directly on the Internet twenty-four hours a day. Nine cameras operate constantly in the living room, kitchen, game room and in each of the bedrooms in the first floor. [...] They can be moved at will to film in the smaller nooks and crannies of the house. Lamps and projectors arranged all over the place furnish a diffuse light, guaranteeing a clear image day and night. The soundtrack is made with the same care.

Here we are indeed in the "house of glass" to which everyone has access and can even engage directly in dialogue with the occupants, *via* a direct channel. These people submit to the game quickly. Thus Sharon always arranges things to show "her face up close while she sleeps" and, she says,

> I always do this when I go to bed, it is important, our visitors need to know who we are, it makes Here & Now an in-

---

[100] Yves Eudes, *Le Monde*, 28 April 2000, p. 16-17.

timate experience [...]. I consider all the people who hook up
to be invited by me, I speak to them and attend to them as
though they were physically next to us.

Revealing still earlier that it is hardly possible to have private conversations in such a context, the journalist asks
Sharon "What do you think of all this: is the right to privacy
nothing more than the right to opacity? Will Here & Now put
us under the oppressive surveillance of our surroundings, or
on the contrary, help us free ourselves from the making of
secrets?"

A moral dimension

The response of the inhabitants of the house of glass is
astonishing. It plunges us right away into a universe of profound justifications that makes clear to us the nature of the
belief in transparence that the Internet permits. Sharon re-
sponded thus: "I am one of those people who can have an
intimate conversation about anything at all. I have nothing to
hide from my friends, nor from my parents. I will never do
anything to be ashamed of, with or without a camera." Joe,
another occupant of the house who had, as Yves Eudes said,
"opted for transparency," added: "My life is simple; I do not
like to lie. [...] What this is about is that we are the pioneers of
a movement that will grow. [...] Soon, many people will live
like us, above all young people."

Transparence is also—especially?—a moral transparence:
to have nothing to hide is to not commit a sin. The simple
fact that an act, a word—a thought?—is made visible suffices
to make it morally acceptable. What is hidden, whatever its
nature may be, because it is hidden, is sinful, morally repre-
hensible. Here is one measure of the importance of the
change of values that the new religiosity brings about.

Transparence is also ubiquity: to be both here and over
there at the same time, permanently. While waiting for gen-

eral interconnectivity, the director of the project, Erik, first imagined that,

> If a half dozen houses equipped like this one were intercon-
> nected (in the whole world), we could create a space that
> would be both real and virtual at the same time, completely
> novel. [...] We would see and hear ourselves constantly, as if
> we inhabited one and the same place. The true promise of
> the Internet is the power to be in many places simultane-
> ously, to live many parallel lives.

It is curious to note that not once in the article does Yves Eudes ask or answer the question of what the purpose of such a project is. (Moreover, funding for the project is not mentioned). Its purpose is clear throughout the narrative: it is nothing less than to put into operation, to actualize, transpar-ence. But why do that? There one runs into the wall of belief, which is not explained, not argued, but is seen, felt, and mani-fests itself. Transparence is a postulate, an element of faith.

This experience is not unique. Before the project existed, the internauts had already communicated with each other about addresses of sites where with ridiculously feeble techni-cal means (the little cameras which one connects to the Web and which allow one to be seen by the whole world cost scarcely a few hundred francs), some people had already de-cided to "live in public." Indeed one sees that the expression "public" is itself obsolete in this context: it refers to a pri-vate/public distinction that no longer exists in the world of transparence.

The rejection of the distinction between private and pub-lic life corresponds to the belief in the virtues of a social life entirely collective, where a person has nothing to hide. Within such a belief, persons are less individuals endowed with their own interiority than collective "informational beings."

Free circulation and the rejection of the Law

For the fundamentalists of the Internet, the ideal of a transparent world is realized in the "global village," without frontiers, without Law, without constraint. "Free circulation" is in effect a leitmotiv among the "globalists." The argument for transparence thus poses, one thing leading to another, in its more profound replies, the question of the Law and of social and juridical norms. What is the place of Law in such a system? The Law is at the same time both the authority that regulates conflict and the guide to behavior. It is at the same time right and morality. The basis of the Law never appears clearly to us. It is a hidden third party. It supposes the constraint by the third party that imposes itself on all parties. For the fundamentalists, the Law is the antithesis of transparence.

The rejection of the Law goes hand in hand with a taste—often immoderate—for the rule, the procedure, the algorithm, that adequately describes a problem and permits the "self-regulation" (another key notion) of its resolution. Norbert Wiener regularly fulminated against what he called the "negatively phototropic fauna of the courts" (yet another solar metaphor!). He thus translates into his own terms the sentiment held by many in informatics circles that the law and justice are arbitrary, given over to questionable judicial procedures and the rhetoric of speech, whereas a good description of the problem in terms of information allows for "nonarbitrary" and incontestable solutions. In the new cult of the Internet, rule replaces the Law and self-regulation replaces the norm. The ideal resolution of a problem rests in the algorithm.

The attack on the Law, against the very idea of Law, takes form through the assertion that cyberspace by nature must be free from the "constraints" of national and even international laws. Cyberspace will be another world where old things will no longer have any currency, where one can "enjoy oneself without restraint" in any manner whatsoever, without disturbing others.

Nonetheless, this view poses a problem: how to do away with violence and the Law at the same time? We shall see that the solution to this dilemma is social separation, which will presumably suppress all violence while limiting recourse to the Law.

Is law applicable to the Internet?

Since the emergence of the Internet, meetings, seminars and colloquia are all abuzz with the same question that would be astonishing in any other context: does the law apply to the Internet? It seems that, even today, the advocates of a negative response to that question have carried the day. National laws are judged to be ill adapted to that supranational space which is the Internet.

Isabelle Falque-Pierrotin, master of petitions in the Conseil d'État in France remarks that "two conceptions appear to oppose each other: the supporters of state interventionism and classical regulation, and the apostles of self-regulation." That last position, the dominant one, supports itself through the "sacralization of freedom of expression in the United States," compared to the "Latin system that appeals to the exigencies of public order."[101]

It is difficult to locate the defense of the Internet as a space of non-law in the understanding of youth, in the novelty of it, or in the Americanization of the world (even if it is a vector of the latter). It is indeed a question of taking a strong position dictated by the belief in an ideal of the "systematic free circulation" of information. Rather than considering it to be a matter of the imperialistic extension of an

---

[101] Isabelle Falque-Pierrotin, "Quelle régulation pour Internet et les réseaux?" *Le Monde, Horizons-Débats,* 27 November, 1999.

American conception, one should consider that the militants of free circulation rely opportunistically on an American political value that, in the name of freedom of communication, rejects all intervention of the law in that area.

The importance of this point of view for the Internet is that here is its weakest link, for one has access, in North America, to all sorts of sites in which the content is against the law in other countries, for example sites expressing revisionist theses. (But this particular example should not be the tree that hides the forest and it is necessary to guard against all confusions.) Even if, to protect the freedom of circulation, numerous internauts are prepared to protect such contents if their dissemination is threatened (and this we do see) they do so evidently not due to sympathy for such ideas but from an almost religious hatred of censorship.

The rejection of censorship

Pierre Lévy wrote "Thanks to the end of censorship and cultural monopolies, everything which consciousness can explore is rendered visible to everyone."[102] Not hesitating to use religious metaphors, Negroponte, for whom "the law of copyright is completely outdated," added that

> There is simply no way to limit the freedom of bit radiation, any more than the Romans could stop Christianity, even though a few brave and early data broadcasters may be eaten by the Washington lions in the process.[103]

The pirating and widest possible diffusion of music or text otherwise protected by copyright law is therefore considered as an absolute necessity and even a moral duty by those who defend the virtues of open networks. "Will the rights of

---

[102] Pierre Lévy, *World philosophie, op. cit.*, p. 175.
[103] Nicholas Negroponte, *Being digital, op. cit.*, p. 55-56.

the author survive the Internet?"[104] The question is not just theoretical. One is tempted to add: "Will authors survive the Internet?" Even in Europe the states are divided on the necessity of defending those rights, France remaining very isolated. Yet, Viviane Reding, European commissioner in charge of this matter, acknowledged,

> If nothing is done, there may be a catastrophe. This is what is happening to music on the Internet with the multiplication of pirate copies. That the same thing should happen with books or film absolutely must be avoided.[105]

Ignoring copyright law implies—this point is rarely emphasized—a very great value judgment concerning the nature of the work itself. The fundamentalist ethos implies in effect that the value of a work lies in its potential for communication and disclosure. An author who reserves to himself some rights regarding access will see his work immediately disqualified by that simple fact, for the "true" creation is known by the fact of its being open. The content matters less than ever, only the capacity of the form of display.

So the texts which circulate on the Internet, assumed to be potential bringers of "world salvation," become more and more fragmented—due to the exigencies of interactivity—and less and less points of reference. That tendency also appears clearly among the authors coming from the world of the new information technologies who, like Pierre Lévy, do not hesitate to write an entire book in which the direct influence of numerous authors is evident, with hardly any citations, references or notes. The principle is without doubt that in order for ideas to be "open" and circulate more freely it is

---

[104] See the article by Véronique Mortaigne and Nicole Vurser, "La difficile défense des droits d'auteur sur Internet," *Le Monde*, 31 May 2000, p. 23.
[105] Interview with Nicole Vurser, *Le Monde*, 31 May 2000, p. 23.

no longer necessary to shackle them with such ridiculous trappings as references to their sources.

This realignment of behavior of many internauts, who are in fact acting illegally by copying and disseminating CDs, books, and software, allows them to avoid seeing themselves as willful delinquents and profiteers. Instead, in their own eyes they occupy the high moral ground. One thus finds everywhere what would otherwise be considered as calls for delinquency, such as the heading in the march 2000 issue of the official Yahoo! journal *Internet Life*: "The web supplants the music stores, albums available on the web before their distribution," and noted that the "latest trick for those crazy for MP3" (which allows one to download music on the Internet) is to "get albums well before they arrive in the record stores." The article mentions examples of groups (Oasis, Smashing Pumpkins) where pirate copies "made their appearance completely illegally on the servers."[106] The article was written in a tone that left no doubt what the author felt about such practices.

It is not difficult to find the addresses of the servers in question. That culture of free circulation is such that some software vendors do not even hesitate to give out the addresses where one can download—for free of course—some of the software which they are themselves selling on their sites. Negroponte wrote "We will see a new kind of fraud appear, which may not be fraud at all."[107]

Hacking—the secret side of the cult

Not many of the usual categories of classical criminology are applicable for understanding the behavior of the "hackers" who regularly attack Internet sites. Thus, describing the

---

[106] Article signed by B.G., *Yahoo! Internet Life*, March 2000, p. 15.
[107] Nicholas Negroponte, *Being Digital, op. cit.*, p. 59.

very effective raids which targeted large sites like Amazon or Yahoo! in early 2000, Laure Belot and Enguérand Renault note that according to "the spokespersons for these sites, [...] the attacks did not have as their object breaking into the information system to steal confidential data: no credit card numbers were taken, no confidential files were violated."[108] Only the active cult of transparence, of openness, of the abolition of the secret explains such behavior (even if, certainly, old style delinquents indifferent to the mystique use the Internet as a tool just as in the beginning of the last century they scrambled to learn locksmithing).

Hacking is truly the secret dimension of the cult of the Internet, the activity of those who hide themselves to make the world more transparent. Biographies of hackers are rare. They always reveal practically the same profile: the "fascination with the secret." "I am always opening everything," one of them tells Pascale Nivelle, "video games, vacuum cleaners—one can disassemble a vacuum cleaner to the last bolt and no one will care, but not a cash machine." This last speaker who had cracked the codes of the *Carte Bleue* in 1999 went on to offer a self-portrait: "My state of mind isn't based on nothing, like a motor that purrs. I am continually educating myself. I arrange everything, my clothes, my ideas! That really helps to live life in this kind of secrecy."[109]

The biographies of these passionate lovers of the Internet often show two traits, beyond the world of the "hackers": first, a pronounced and precocious taste (often from infancy) for objects and above all material objects, a taste which is precisely expressed by a will to take apart those objects, to render them transparent; and second, the future amateur en-

---

[108] Laure Belot and Enguérand Renault, "Les attaques sur le Net ébranlent la nouvelle économie," *Le Monde*, 11 February 2000.
[109] Pascale Nivelle, *Libération*, 25 February 2000. ["Blue cards" refers to a French banking "smartcard."—translator]

gineers generally have a shizoid personality, that is to say, a tendency to lack a desire for contact with others. From these two points of view, our hackers are indeed in the image of the world of the Internet believers.

How should one consider computer viruses? There, also, it is indeed the world of beliefs developed around the Internet that permits one to see something other than simply an aberration, or gratuitous acts of pure delinquency. The reality is more complex. If one analyzes viruses by taking into account the paradigm we describe here, we discover that viruses are not special or marginal products: they are programs like the others, even closer to normalcy. In effect, the virus—technically, small pieces of software—is the prototype of a program which circulates most easily and is constructed so as to get around whatever obstacles may get in its way. From the point of view of the belief in the freest possible circulation, this is the best software there is.

One study done a few years ago among information scientists showed a very weak attachment of professionals in this area to the values of information security, and instead, a strong belief that "information systems should remain as open as possible."[110]

Internet fundamentalists are not hostile to the Law, they simply believe it does not pertain to them. They do not oppose it in the name of any revolution; they simply deny the law's pertinence in the regulation of social relations. Some of them, dissatisfied with the direction that the Internet has taken, recently imagined constructing another network. According to Yves Eudes, a young English computer programmer named Ian Clarke imagined an underground-network "capable of guaranteeing freedom of expression better than the Web." "My philosophy is simple," he explained, "I think

[110] Philippe Breton, "L'informaticien et la sécurité: enquête sur un antagonisme," *Les cahiers de la sécurité intérieure*, Paris, 1996.

all censorship is wrong, without exception, whatever the intention. Freedom of expression must be absolute." This concerns "everything quantifiable" in the world, including music. "Musicians who try to impede the free copying of their works are behind the times, they do not understand the dynamics of the network."[111] Already a rumor has circulated for some time: below the Internet there is another network where, in secret, the whole world is free... What a paradox for a world of transparence!

Direct communication, or the rejection of mediation

This belief in the virtues of a disincarnate and collectivist universe implies that in the interior of the "new world" information circulates unconstrained. We have seen that law and norm constitute a form of opacity that is especially rejected. There are other obstacles to any communication that a fundamentalist internaut wants to be as "direct" as possible; every form of mediation from beginning to end is just as insupportable in that universe. The middlemen, as intermediaries, are a restraint to the free circulation of information and to the transparence of the new world. At least four large areas of social activity illustrate that belief: commerce, education, media and politics.

In these four areas, when the taste for unlimited transparence and openness has come up against the concrete realities of our world, entire professions have been denigrated, accused of "resisting change," and of being a part of the "old world." Their rapid disappearance is called progress.

Electronic commerce

In the area of commerce, as elsewhere, one finds a separation between the Internet as tool and the Internet as cult. The

---

[111] Yves Eudes, *Le Monde*, 29 May 2000, p. 37.

new information technologies did not invent mail order sales, even though one can speak of their role in the modernization of the practice. The network could be a formidable tool for that original form of commerce, adapting it to certain wishes or certain situations. But the cult of the Internet places the question of commerce into a completely different perspective, the two perspectives having no common ground. Briefly, why not purchase everything by yourself? When there are so many occasions to meet "in spirit," why lose time uselessly moving the body about, part of which effort is devoted to nourishing what David Le Breton refers to as a "supernumerary" body?

In addition to that fundamental reason, articulated according to the belief in the inanity of physical encounter, there is another equally profound reason: the more commerce is direct, unmediated, the more open and profitable the game should be. Here one finds the original matrix of transparence: the "intermediary," above all the physical intermediary, represents the worst opacity that can be. In the area of books for example, the bookshop is particularly referred to as a physical place where one can choose, get advice, purchase or order a book not in stock. Compared to that, all the possibilities offered by the "on-line bookstore" dazzles the internaut. Yet these possibilities all boil down to a single function: ordering books, although with the added possibility of home delivery.[112]

Teaching

In education, the most radical voices do not hesitate to argue that traditional instruction must rapidly disappear since all knowledge is potentially "on line" and available on the

---

[112] [Home delivery, of course, was unheard of prior to and perhaps only made possible by the Internet—translator.]

Internet. The role of the teacher tends to pass from a face-to-face to a side-by-side-in-front-of-the-screen pedagogy. For the secretary general of the SGEN-CFDT, one of the principal teachers' unions in France, teachers will be transformed into "knowledge engineers, into organizers of the process of the acquisition of knowledge."[113] That vision implies a radical transformation of the actual role of the professor and of the coming end of his role as intermediary of knowledge.

Francois Thibault, in charge of the mission of the Sub-Directorate of Technology to the French Ministry of Research, estimates that "The interest in education at a distance is one of responding to a social demand and of changing the university in terms of educational engineering."[114] The change of perspective is made clear with the vocabulary of the engineer replacing that of the educator and with the neo-liberal lexicon replacing that of public service. It is estimated that the "education market" will be 90 billion dollars in 2005, and that the first "World Education Market" (WEM) conference that took place in Vancouver on the 24th to the 27th of May 2000 brought together 3000 professionals. Claude Moreau, head of continuing education at the Université de technologie de Compiègne, remarked rather crudely that "We are businesses, but we remain profoundly marked by our culture of public service. We have not admitted that education is a business."[115]

Why remain together in places of education called schools, lyceums, or universities? That "archaism" must give way to the promise that the networks offer ("more knowledge"), on the condition that we separate ourselves and renounce these institutions of face-to-face encounter. This

---

[113] Cited by Michel Alberganti, *Le Monde*, 8 December 1999, p. 29.
[114] Cited by Sandrine Blanchard, "Le premier marché mondial de l'éducation s'est ouvert à Vancouver," *Le Monde*, 26 May 2000.
[115] *Ibid.*

revolution is not concerned only with the place where knowledge is transmitted, but knowledge itself, transformed by the fact of being "on-line"—unless putting knowledge on-line is not a pretext for still more profound changes. The representation of knowledge, thus conditioned and formatted in the form of a single dimension—information—approaches an ideal encyclopedia where the separate entities are combinable and recomposable ad infinitum.

Splendidly expressing and theorizing the point of view of the "new education market," which extols the maximum development of "knowledge on line," Pierre Lévy announced that soon

> [T]here will be more and more of a concurrence between on-line and local universities, then between the universities on-line when many local universities have been obliged to close [...]. It is equally possible that the global universities, after a series of sales and mergers, will not be more than four or five in the whole world, like the automobile, insurance or communications corporations [...]. The examination systems will be automated.[116]

Between the producers of knowledge—more and more numerous and splintered, obedient to the rules of the "collective consciousness"—and the consumer, there is no need for an intermediary. The on-line school dispenses with the need for any encounter with a now useless mediator and with equally-useless other students. After the traditional face-to-face education, the side-by-side-in-front-of-the-computer style in turn gives way to the "one-on-one" with the screen.

The new journalism

This process of the disqualification of middlemen plays out equally in the news media. The ideal of transparence and

---

[116] Pierre Lévy, *World philosophie, op. cit.*, p. 96.

free circulation implies the diminution, and in the end, suppression, of that obstacle that the journalist and the journal
represent. The cult of the Internet brought about the emergence of a "new" journalism that makes less of a big deal
about the real. As the author of an article in the *New York
Times* remarked, "What interests today's journalist is no
longer receiving the Pulitzer but to increase the number of
hits on his Internet site."[117] The objective, conforming to the
canons of the new religiosity, is to favor "interactivity." As
Paul-André Tavoillot, an old editor-in-chief of the daily *La
Tribune* which has gone the way of "e-journalism," remarked:
"If the whole world connects to his site, in the short term it
makes little difference in the capacity for creating a bond with
a community of internet users."[118]

   The quality of information no longer lies in its referential
character (the old ideal of objectivity), but in its capacity to
circulate rapidly and to be the most interactive possible. Thus
one of the first founders of an Internet journal, the American
Matt Drudge, became famous for spreading the first information on the relations between the President of the United
States and one of his employees, without having verified it,
and in the name of the principle that the public is big enough
to make allowance for the facts. "I prefer to do everything
myself" he said, "to be able to say what one wants, to press a
key, and that is that. It would be stupid to renounce that."[119]

   In any case, like the businessman and the teacher, the
journalist as middleman is called to disappear from the system: the development of the technologies of surveillance in
public spaces allows each one to see directly what is real,
without intermediaries. Already in certain cities like Mulhouse
in France, the public has access to video-surveillance screens

---

[117] Cited in *Libération*, 16 February 2000, p. 24.
[118] *Ibid.*
[119] Cited by Ignacio Ramonet, *La tyrannie de l'information, op. cit.*, p. 81.

put up throughout the neighborhoods. In the city of glass one can henceforth see everything directly, without intermediary and without risk.

Political representation

The last area exemplifying the rejection of middlemen as obstacles to transparence and free circulation has to do with politicians, insofar as they represent opinion. Conforming to a certain ideal of unimpeded direct communication the political vision of that new world is systematically one of "direct democracy." Representative democracy is judged to be not in conformity with the spirit of the new religiosity.

We have already seen that one of the trumps of the Internet is that it will be able to render governance "transparent." For Jean-Noël Tronc, councilor on new information technologies for the French Prime Minister, the network is the sole means for reforming public administration. And many political parties play the "transparency" card, in the manner of the Communist Party of France, as a sign of the modernization of their activities.

Well beyond these specific uses of a new tool, of that "web-mania that is knocking politics around," there stands out, more radically, an argument against politics in its current forms. The great collectivism of spirits that the Internet permits will authorize direct, rapid, and interactive forms of decision-making that will render obsolete political representation.

The vindication of the spirit, or the rejection of embodied speech

The study of transparence and of the information view of the world arrives, in the first place, at the human being, in his essence, before concerning itself with his being in society. One important part of the intellectual efforts made by the

Internet fundamentalists consists in the construction and imposition of a new representation of the human being. This refers both to what the human being is now and what the human being shall become in the future. The human being is redefined as an "informational being." The influence of Norbert Wiener, of Alan Turing and of the first cyberneticists is immense here. The new view of the human being that this brings forth contributes greatly to defining the ideal portrait of the one who, because he is resolutely devoted to life on the Internet, exalts whatever is suited to it, more open within it.

This new representation of Man leads to a de-centering in comparison to customary representations and practices. It exalts three essential traits: the comparability between human and machine, interactivity, and the privilege given to spirit over the body and interiority. This is indeed a "New Man," who must be valued and constructed, more transparent and more luminous than the old.

The comparability of the human and the machine

We have seen in the previous chapter how this question of the general equivalence of humans and machines that permits a description in terms of information played a founding role in the new cult of information. This possibility of a bridge linking natural man and these artificial beings that are machines is an old project that began with the myth of Galatea and Pygmalion, continuing later in the form of the Golem and numerous automatons, robots, artificial intelligences and other cyborgs.

Behind this theme of artificial creatures that we have analyzed in an earlier work,[120] there stands the idea that humanity is not at the center of the universe, that other kinds of hu-

---

[120] Philippe Breton, *À l'image de l'homme, op. cit.*

manities are possible, resting on foundations other than the human body. This very general vision makes the human being otherwise the equal—this possibility is soon foreseen—or at least the symmetrical partner of computers and other information machines. Thus all are able to claim complexity, consciousness and spirit. Even Hugo de Garis, professor at Starlab in Brussels, who gives himself out to be a "techno-prophet of artificial intelligences and of the robotic," affirms that "humanity is going to have to come to a decision as to whether or not to produce massively intelligent machines that will be immensely superior to us."[121]

If thought is a "program," as many information scientists like Herbert A. Simon insist, it is not out of place in the universe of the information programs that populate the Internet and which are of the same material. A program among programs, the human being is sometimes hardly able to determine whether a person he communicates with on the networks is human or computer software. There we are in the heart of that famous argument which the English mathematician believed would prove that machines could "think." Turing's test, upon which every debate in the fifties focused, was a device that already initiated the idea of intelligences in a network, indeed intelligence by means of the network.

This test, which Turing called the "imitation game,"[122] consisted in a device where a questioner addresses two separate partners in two distinct rooms and asks them all sorts of questions without any direct physical contact with them. If the questioner is not able to tell the difference between the two, then they are fundamentally similar. The first version of the test was applied to the distinction between a man and a woman, the second between a human and a machine, in this

[121] Hugo de Garis, "Fracture idéologique," *Le Monde interactif*, 5 July 2000.
[122] Alan Turing, "Les ordinateurs et l'intelligence," in *Pensée et machine*, Champ-Vallon, coll. "Milieux," Seysel, 1983.

case, a computer. Turing was convinced that soon a computer would be indistinguishable from a human being in the game.

Behind that test was a more fundamental point of view that was described by Turing's biographer Andrew Hodges: "The discrete-state machine [the computer], communicating by teletype alone, was like an ideal for his own life, in which he would be left alone in a room of his own, to deal with the outside world solely by rational argument."[123] That "ideal of life" shows us that the idea of the network, of the human being made by the network, preceded, by far, its concrete realization. Let us imagine for just an instant that Turing's ideal of life were fully realized: this means that just as humans talking among themselves would not know whether they were conversing with another human or with a machine, so machines could not know whether they were addressing a human being or one of their own...

For Turing, who expressed the thinking of the first computer programmers as well as that of the current Internet fundamentalists very well, man and woman, human and computer, all belong, in essence, to the same category, which we have called the "informational androgyne," the being faced with separation, the ideal realization, as well, of the "reunion" which will permit "generalized interconnection."

Privileging the spirit and rejecting the body

We note again that one constant of this cult of the informational being, both its *sine qua non* and the price to be paid for it, is the rejection of the body. As David Le Breton analyzed it, the body is a preferential target of "cyberculture": "A religiosity of the machine is imposed on the basis of a denigration of the human and of a contempt for the bodily condi-

---

[123] Alan Hodges, *Alan Turing: the Enigma*, Vintage, London, 1992, p. 425.

tion which is inherent to it."[124] The body indeed constitutes this dark residue, that source of entropy that permanently holds back the spirit:

> Navigation on the Net or virtual reality gives the internauts the feeling of being shorn of a useless and encumbering body, which must be fed, cared for, entertained, etc., when life is more pleasant without such hindrance. Communication without a face, without flesh, favors multiple identities, the fragmentation of the subject engaged in a series of virtual encounters for which he takes each time a different name, even a different age, sex or profession chosen according to the circumstances. Cyberculture is often described by these adepts as a marvelous world open to the mutants who invent a new universe; this universe is necessarily without a body.[125]

In many science fiction stories, as for example the famous *Neuromancer*[126] by William Gibson, the fallen heroes are condemned to "return to their bodies" and leave the place where the spirits are networked and in constant interconnection. The forgetting or denial of the body returns us to a recurrent theme in the history of artificial creatures, that of imperfection. If one were to work on a being "in the image of man," this latter is imperfect, fragile, mortal; from this point of view the new creature would constitute an immense progress. Disentangled from its materiality, from the opacity of its body, the new being would therefore progress more surely towards the Light.

But whereas the golems, automatons, and other robots oppose the human body to the possibility of another body where the spirit would be better deployed, the new religiosity introduces an important novelty. The classical automaton is

---

[124] David Le Breton, *L'adieu au corps, op. cit.*, p. 190.

[125] *Ibid.*, p. 18.

[126] William Gibson, *Neuromancer*, Ace, New York, 1984.

linked to an individualist conception of the human; that is why it is anthropomorphic. The intelligent network incarnates a figure more in accord with the collectivism of the new cult.

Furthermore, it is because it is the source of individuality that the body is considered as an obstacle to the reunion of spirits in the same information entity. "In fact," Pierre Lévy tells us in a strong formulation, "ideas circulate in us; we are their vehicles, even though we have the impression that we think them."[127] This conception, largely inspired by Teilhard de Chardin, and in which mysticism is clearly the living core, is however mixed with Eastern philosophy, especially with Buddhist inspiration. The spirit, once it has been disengaged from the weighty body/spirit dualism, is headed for another destiny:

> All the more intelligent than the harnessed forms are the universal, the impersonal. In other words, the more the spirit is emptied (of ego or partiality) the better it can harness form. Up to the universal form par excellence, that which has no form yet contains them all.[128]

The study of the "emptying of thought" is inscribed in the "path of deliverance" opened by the Buddha (deliverance from the body) but also, it is often forgotten, an emptying of the spirit.

Individuality, interiority, speech, "charged with special intentions, messengers of personal meaning," which, according to Georges Gusdorf, do not intervene in order to facilitate human relations but "constitute them,"[129] have hardly any place in the cult of information and transparence. That defense of the light, the old metaphor of interiority, that inner

---

[127] Pierre Lévy, *World philosophie, op. cit.*, p. 191.

[128] *Ibid.*, p. 122.

[129] George Gusdorf, *La parole*, PUF, Paris, 1952, p. 5-7.

space partially hidden from the individual who carries it and which, from St. Augustine to Freud, determines his essential actions, finds no favor at all here.

Transparence, as an article of faith, is a subversion of the axis of interiority/exteriority. There can indeed be, in appearance, a visible exterior and a hidden interior, but from the moment that everything is knowable onward, the interior always passes potentially to the exterior: it is reversible, "like a glove." What is the human being? A being completely turned towards the exterior, "phototropic," that realizes itself only through abandoning the imaginary individual crypt.

Interactivity, or the rejection of the embodied speech

In this context, the status of speech constitutes a fundamental issue. Speech is conceived as being purged only of certain of its essential dimensions, notably those that connect it to interiority. The key notion here is that of "interactivity," mostly used to designate a practical ideal: everything must be "interactive" and whatever is not is doomed to the pillory.

One example among a thousand, the "new relation" to music that the new technologies permit: "We attract musicians," says Graham Browne Martin, "by asking them to go for broader communication. The new generation does not have the same approach to the media; it has grown up with video, interactive games, multiple channels and channel hopping. It does not want to remain captive; it wants to participate, to engage its spirit. Music is a passive experience, and if one wishes to increase its power of attraction, it is necessary to give power to the hearer, permitting him to control his environment."[130]

The following paragraphs include several of the commonplaces that are used to describe interactivity. First,

---

[130] Interview in *Libération*, 29-30 January 1994.

though, a qualification: music, so far, has not been a "passive experience." It is indeed the imagination and the interiority of listening which are noted here as a sign of passivity. Now, a new development: the capacity to actively intervene in the received message is part of the message.

The technical mechanism that lies behind the abstract notion of interactivity is a notion well known to information specialists: feedback, the "retroaction" revealed by Wiener's theory. Human speech, human activity in general is thus redefined as a "reaction to a reaction," according to Gregory Bateson, or, in the words of Pierre Lévy, "the ultra-sensible seismograph of a society of seismographs that register each other."[131]

That purely informational speech lacks two other dimensions of human speech, excluding them: the expressive and argumentative capacities, both tied to individuality and interiority, to the singularity of an opinion or of a view of the world. But for the Internet fundamentalists, this loss is all relative, since, as Pierre Lévy frankly states,

> The illusion of individual thought is "idiocy" par excellence. [...] The individual is an intermediary articulation, transitory, certainly no more important than the species, culture, lineage, the situation, the moment. [...] The illusion of the I is a "gimmick" of natural selection, very useful for the reproduction of our species in its prehistoric environment but which has now lost its usefulness.[132]

As if in echo, Timothy Leary indicated that "in a near future, the human being as we now know him, that perishable creature, will be no more than a simple historical curiosity, a relic, a ridiculous point lost in a world of an unimaginable diversity of forms."[133] One could not be clearer.

---

[131] Pierre Lévy, *World philosophie, op. cit.*, p. 46.

[132] *Ibid.*, p. 201.

[133] Timothy Leary, cited by David Le Breton, *op. cit.*, p. 215.

The notion of interactivity in fact serves to designate a collection of practices that their authors would call "collectivist" if they were not afraid of the negative connotations acquired by that word from communism. Interactivity permits "communicational continuity," and situates actions no longer in reference to an alternation of inner attention and social confrontation, but rather as set in a permanent mingling where the collective does not allow any opening for the individual.

Indeed that is where the mystical dream of Teilhard de Chardin leads, though he could not have imagined exactly how things would come to pass. He was not far from the Internet when, in the 1950s, he imagined a "noosphere, an immense thinking machine," where the personality would no longer live isolated, but would form a "super-organism." The great mystic concluded: "The collectivization weaves itself little by little; it is irresistible since it expresses the human aspiration towards increasing consciousness."[134]

But the price of interactivity, of the new collectivism to which a number of internauts actively strive, is, as we shall see later on, the renunciation of encounter, of physical presence, of the exchange of spoken words.

---

[134] Cited by Georges Magloire and Hubert Cuypers, *Teilhard de Chardin,* Éditions universitaires, Paris, 1964.

5.

The foundations of the new religiosity

How was the Internet-for-everything religion, that mystique of information, of communication, of message and social transparence, so thoroughly and so rapidly diffused throughout society? The first reason for that success pertains to the fact that the new religiosity based itself upon (at the same time as it contributed to the development of) what was generally regarded as a good tool.

The Internet is in effect an innovation in the area of communication technology, continuing in the line of the invention of writing and of printing. Although they are not free from rigidity and there are severe limits on their use, information devices and the network are powerful tools, appreciated by everyone except the most radical technophobes whose opposition is a question of principle. Without the Internet, the new faith under discussion would have had great difficulty spreading. The existence of the Internet and the orientation that the new information mystique succeeded in giving to it forms the background for the success of its ideology. But that is not the only reason.

The cult of the Internet appears as a vast, patched-together construction, supported on elements translated from the worlds of values, religion, culture and politics. These elements are at the same time its environment and base of propagation. The new conjunction between classical liberalism and the heritage of the "counter-culture" is not without effect on its current success. The context of crisis and change for the grand worldviews of humanism and monotheism, the shocks and deep ruptures that the social bond has experienced, make a favorable background for the acceptability of this new faith. One must add to this that the Internet militants use not only every tactic of direct persuasion but also certain forms of propaganda, especially directed toward youth.

We shall attempt to disentangle the different skeins of a success that grows each day more invasive, by beginning with the proximity of the new religiosity to other older religious values.

Of closely related religious themes

One immediately notes that the "modernity" of the cult of the Internet is particularly indebted to the old, indeed very conservative, character of certain currents of thought that both are close to it and serve to spread it. Without being intimately familiar with this world, everyone knows very well that between the new religiosity and old values, new connections continue to be established. How can we not look into the many links that exist between the Internet fundamentalists and certain Buddhist schools, or the various currents of the "New Age"? How could one fail to see in the relation to the movement that we shall describe, very old connections with puritan influences, even of hygienics? How could we not see that a Manichean or Gnostic vision of the world nourishes that ideal of a society where light comes to chase away evil? And how can we avoid seeing the influence and imprint of that world-view systematized by Teilhard de Chardin?

As we have seen in the case of Steve Jobs, the Zen movement had many followers among those in the world of the new technologies, even though their number cannot be precisely measured. Today, many of the philosophers of cyberspace have converted to some form of mysticism in order to harmonize their vision of the future world society with a foundation of older values.

A non-deist cult

The cult of information has apparently united several currents of thought in order to form this new composite where the religiosity that is affirmed takes new and original forms. Right away we must make it clear that in the group of texts analyzed here, it never follows that this religiosity is in any way deist (which does not mean that some of the followers may not, under whatever name, believe in God or in some divinity).

Divinities have little place in the universe of the new technologies, and are also absent in the global information society. The new religiosity is perhaps even atheist, or at least indifferent to the idea of God. It is also, in a certain fashion, hostile to the idea of religion in the usual sense that supposes a certain institutionalization and a centralism at odds with the idea of dispersed networks. In no part of any of the texts saturated with the new religiosity can one find a divine figure. In this sense, it is a deviation from the heritage of Teilhard de Chardin, who remained within the Christian faith and associated his "noosphere" with God (and with the Catholic Church, to the point that in the name of his faith he willingly observed the silence imposed upon him by his Order).

All the same, the theme of good and evil is very evident in the new cult. There is no God in it, but we have met the Devil several times, most notably in Norbert Wiener's work. Is he a metaphorical Devil? That is not at all clear. The beliefs that we have analyzed seem to refer to a definite weakening of monotheism or of deism, without in the least taking away from the importance of Evil and those who embody it. The Internet imagination is overflowing with obscure forces, which are, just because they are obscure, and often only for that reason, in the end, on the Devil's side.

We shall set out a few markers in order to try to indicate the terrain, more or less precisely, or more or less impression-istically. Here the links are tenuous, difficult to establish. One elaborates on parallels, on objective convergences rather than on precise relationships that one could establish sociologi-cally.

The shadow of Teilhard de Chardin

First of all it is necessary to return to the amazing proxim-ity of the thought of Teilhard de Chardin to the new cult. That thought in a way remained "suspended in air" since his desire to be done with the "separation of human beings" and his proposals of "collectivism" and the "noosphere" had no concrete basis for their elaboration. The encounter between the famous Jesuit's philosophy and cybernetics, even though they were of the same era, did not come about immediately.

"Teilhardism," one among several tentative reconciliations of science and religion, saturated the imagination of an age given to reflections on "cosmic" nature. The history of that influence has yet to be written, and it will have to suffice to say that Pierre Lévy, in spite of his importance today, claims that lineage, so that one can credibly connect it with the whole milieu.

Teilhard was not far from being considered a heretic, and what is more, his Order forced him into partial silence. He affirmed, in fact, "man is not the only receptacle of the Word." (The fictional work on this theme by Jean-Michel Truong makes interesting reading.[135]) That fundamental break with the dogmas which made man the center of the world

---

[135] Jean-Michel Truong, *Le successeur de Pierre*, Denoël, Paris, 1999.

here below brought his thought near the anti-humanism at work in the new religiosity.

He also vigorously defended a cosmic vision of the world where "consciousness" seeks its way, through matter, then through life, until it reaches the ultimate good. His point of view is similar to a dualism as well as to the new cult of information. All of this is written in the context of an older tradition, a body of doctrines that, while quite heterogenous, have in common the opposition of an intelligible world and a sensible world, of a world of ideas and forms and of a material world, which to a great extent passes the boundaries of Gnosticism.

Gnosticism, Manicheism, Dualism

One finds that this opposition, initially formulated by Plato, flowed into numerous philosophical currents, and, much later, was diffused throughout Western culture. It is also at work in "Gnosticism," and on this subject David Le Breton comments that "the Gnostic religiosity escaped into its many doctrinal forms; one now meets it again in a more powerful secular form in certain elements of techno-science."[136]

Is the cult of the Internet a Gnosticism, or perhaps related to that tradition, only traces or diluted influences of which remain in contemporary cultures? We recall that Gnosticism (particularly active in the early years of the Christian era—for example it is mentioned in the first Epistle to the Corinthians) is a doctrine, or a group of doctrines, of salvation through knowledge. The Christian Church is hostile to Gnosticism because for the latter perfection and salvation are obtained without moral effort.

---

[136] David Le Breton, *L'adieu au corps, op. cit.*, p. 9.

Interestingly, one finds indications of "pass-words" necessary for crossing frontiers guarded by angels in some ancient
texts dating from the first centuries after Jesus Christ.[137] And
Gnosticism is not exempt from a certain egalitarianism, since
one of its proponents, Isidore, had taught a communism in
regard to goods and women. However, he did not draw very
bold conclusions from those points.

The cult of the Internet is closest to the old Gnostic theories not in the contents of the complex religious stories which
these latter propose, in which one can find no concrete links
to modernity, but in their common manner of "feeling themselves in the world," of the desire to be rid of the body in
order to free the spirit, and of seeing the universe as a conflict of two forces: information and entropy. As Michel Tardieu and Pierre Hadot remind us, citing the description given
by H. C. Puech:

> The main feeling of the Gnostic consists in feeling himself a
> "stranger" to this world. He feels his situation of being-in-
> the-world as abnormal, as violent: the body, the sensible
> world, is a prison, a place dominated by evil and passions.
> The Gnostic has the impression of being in a prison the
> walls of which are on the other side of the stars. [...] The
> Gnostic intensely feels the distinction between his "I" and
> the rest of his being, between the soul and the body. He
> feels himself to be of a different essence. He thinks that he
> belongs to a transcendent world, to a Nature that is a com-
> plete stranger to the world here below.[138]

In some respects Gnosticism is close to the dualist tradition and especially to Manichean conceptions. These latter
suppose that the soul has fallen into the body, but that it can
be delivered by salvation and by knowledge. The Manicheans
(under the influence of Mani, founder of that Church in the

---

[137] Michel Tardieu et Pierre Hadot, "Gnose," *Encyclopaedia universalis*.
[138] *Ibid.*

third century of our era) imagined a world where the "Shadows" gave up fighting the light and where everything must be done so that the particles of light can release themselves from the Shadows and return to their source. Many rituals, including eating rituals, accompanied these beliefs, such as the importance given to food containing "luminous particles."[139]

It is clearly necessary to transpose these themes beyond those times and cultures, with all the risks that that entails. Nevertheless, one can find there a community of subjective feelings among those who do not feel at ease until the tensions of the body are released and the lines of communication that will connect them with others are activated, for an adventure where the content of what is exchanged matters less than the permanent connection to cyberspace. Nearer to current preoccupations, the militants of the Internet are often caught in the web of a diffuse religiosity which was the spirit at the heart of the counter-culture of the sixties, and where the signs of Buddhism, especially of Zen Buddhism, are clearly present.

The continuity with the 60s counter-culture

It would be difficult not to see the connections between the new cult and the widespread counter-culture movement that became a mass phenomenon during the sixties in the United States. We should remember that what we call the "counter-culture"—supposing a homogeneity far greater than the actual facts—is a wide current that lumps together the heritage of the "Beat Generation," the protest movement of youth which led to the great student revolts, the hippie movement, and all the numerous offshoots born in that constellation, such as the "alternative" movements.

---

[139] Henri-Charles Puech, "Manichéisme," *Encyclopaedia universalis.*

The counter-culture movement disappeared as such in the seventies. The values that it carried were nevertheless disseminated and influenced the way of "being-in-the-world" of many adults. Several famous names in the United States remain associated with that flaring up which marked the whole era with its imprint: Alan Ginsburg, Jack Kerouac, Alan Watts, Ken Kesey, Timothy Leary, Gary Snyder, Neal Cassady, Bob Dylan, not to mention the many musical groups and magazines. San Francisco and the West Coast were the privileged places for that "cultural revolution." These movements were continued after the new ideas crossed the Atlantic into Europe.

The European movements were characterized, following the times and circumstances, at once by a protest against the established system and by the establishment of a "parallel culture" and alternative lifestyles. Southern Europe was more contentious whereas northern Europe became more "alternative." In a general way, for the adepts of the counter-culture, the utopia of a better world could be made here and now, all at once—the opposite of the revolutionaries for whom the better world is always the tomorrow of a "great night."

In fact, the practices of the counter-culture led its devotées through a break with the world: (the "dropout"); the initiatory voyage, like the least mendicant Buddhists, most often to India but also along the roads of America and Europe; life in communes; a profound desire for equality on a libertarian basis; the attachment, under the influence of Gandhi, to a culture of non-violence; a closeness to nature; and a certain mysticism tinged with Eastern influences, especially Buddhist (many of the key players in that period converted to Zen Buddhism or joined sects influenced by Eastern philosophy). Society must be conceived as a peaceful community; love and altruism occupy an important place. A vast "underground" was formed involving hundreds of thousands of people in many networks, producing music, books, leisure, food and alternative medicines.

That idea of a new world has indeed many points in common with the contemporary movements surrounding the Internet, which mobilizes, in turn, hundreds of thousands of young people in search of a more brotherly, more "communicating," more peaceful society. The continuity of themes is striking: the world of the Internet is "underground" in its own way; it is the real underground, the place that allows one to leave the "ordinary world." The one who dedicates his time to the Internet is the "drop out" of today, and many descriptions of young internauts entirely absorbed by this new cult present them in a manner strikingly similar to the "Dharma bums" of whom Kerouac spoke.

The heritage of the New Age

Where in the fifties one "hit the road" to find a new meaning for one's life through a different kind of spiritual perspective, today one surfs the "information highway." The analogies are numerous, and, across that continuity, it is always the post-war period that speaks to us, in a kind of fixity that poorly hides the repetition of the forms, as if our society had been stopped there and we replay, in different costumes, the very same scenario.

Timothy Leary well illustrates that continuity. The guru of counter-cultural mysticism and an apostle of the use of LSD to free the mind, he became the guru of the Web, preacher of the Internet, which will free the spirit from the body and create a new community.

The "New Age" movement, parallel to the counter-culture, is already now a powerful arm of the new cult. This movement is a heterogeneous *mélange* of animism and pseudo-scientific theories of "auras" and "energies," of "bio-magnetism," "spiritual technologies" often based on hallucinogenic mushrooms or mind-altering drugs. Electronics early on had an important place in the practice of magic. The New Age, which has many followers in the United States, today includes many more or less folkloric groups who have turned to the Internet as a new support for religiosity.

Marc Dery describes at length some of these different tendencies, such as "techno-paganism" and "cyberdelia." Techno-paganism is the "encounter between paganism (a term that covers a whole range of contemporary religions of a polytheist character) and the New Age on the one hand, and on the other, the digital technologies and the parallel culture of informatics."[140] The number of its followers has grown to between one hundred and three hundred thousand in the United States, "almost all of them white." One of the obsessions of the movement is to "expand consciousness," especially through the network.

Cyberdelia, of which Douglas Rushkoff is the chief exponent, "reconciles the transcendentalists of the sixties' counter-culture and the infomania of the nineties."[141] Thus one speaks of zippies (Zen-inspired Pagan Professionals). The "Gaia Hypothesis," which is the belief in a progressive awakening of the planet, turns up again mixed with the "collective consciousness" of Teilhard de Chardin and the "global village" of McLuhan, all thanks to the wiring of the world that makes the Internet possible, and which will constitute, according to Rushkoff, "the final stage of the development of Gaia."

Robert Pirsig, one of the cult authors of the sixties, had this to say: "The Buddha, the godhead, resides quite as comfortably in the circuits of a digital computer or the gears of a cycle transmission as he does at the top of a mountain or in

---

[140] Mark Dery, *Vitesse virtuelle, op. cit.*, p. 61.
[141] *Ibid*, p. 32.

the petals of a flower."[142] The new cult also connects with the values of the market, which were not part of the counter-culture of the sixties. Of the two grand utopias of the second half of the twentieth century—the revolutionary utopia and the counter-cultural utopia—only the latter has survived, and is in some fashion reincarnated in the new cult of the Internet. The counter-culture, while being completely hostile to big capitalism and to the consumer society, was marked by a libertarian tradition at the same time, and still never completely rejected markets. That explains how the cult of the Internet so easily adopted market values.

The connection with classical liberalism

Throughout that period, which lasted for half a century, from the "everything is information" of Wiener in 1942 until the current "Internet-for-everything," the new religiosity found itself faced with three great currents of thought: the counter-cultural pole, the free market pole, and what we could call the "statist pole."

The counter-cultural pole, which is by nature hardly represented politically, exercised nevertheless a certain influence on American society and other Western societies, especially since the sixties. Certain characteristics of that current immediately resonated with the new thinking about information. We have seen that the society of communication imagined by Wiener is a society without a state, self-regulating thanks to the new technologies which permit free expression, unhampered and unmediated. These theories are finally not far from those of Bakunin, the anarchist thinker of the end of the 19th century, who had already defended "networks" and the "horizontality of social relations."

---

[142] Robert Pirsig, *Zen and the Art of Motorcycle Maintenance*, William Morrow, New York, 1999. p. 26.

Many of the innovators in the area of the new technologies, for example, those who were at the very origin of the invention of the microcomputer in the beginning of the seventies, were a part of some stream of the counter-cultural movement. The computer was conceived as a machine "for the people" which would permit them to fight against capitalism and to establish a counter-culture made of direct democracy and constant change.

The second pole is that of partisans of a "state" usage of the new information technologies, in the framework of the interests of a central power, embodied by the nation state, where the reference to the public interest is always privileged. This tendency has been historically found among those who see military applications as an essential use of the new communication technologies. One should recall that the American mathematician Von Neumann, a "hawk" even more radical than MacArthur, advocated preemptive nuclear bombing of the Soviet Union. The immense possibilities for social control opened up by information technologies were, for him, explicitly or not, the best defense for certain regimes.

On another, very different level, Minitel, the ancestor of the Internet in as far as it was a vast network intended for the public, had been initially conceived by France Télécom, then a state enterprise, as a communication system corresponding to the general public interest. In that spirit the laws passed by the nation state would apply to the information that circulated in the networks, and one could not consider the new communication technologies as extraterritorial. The statist pole is very far from the new religiosity. The secular and military state is not without its own values and will not easily allow itself to be penetrated by an idea of self-regulation and open borders. In it, the new technologies are thought of as tools and not as a lever for making a "new world."

The third pole is formed very classically by the representatives of free market economics. Confident of the laws of the market and hostile to the state intervention that is seen as constraint, these promoters see in the new communication technologies the means for developing the great economic machine by investing in human activities hitherto untouched by market forces. In those areas where education, knowledge, and communication have hitherto escaped the laws of the market, their falling into a vast network of universal communication will permit their transformation into "deposits of profit" for the new entrepreneurs who wish to impose themselves in that domain. The new communication technologies are also the occasion to take back, in a free market capitalist spirit, the prerogative from the state.

Bill Gates, having begun his career in the heart of the counter-culture, and continuing to a degree in its mindset, exemplifies the new generation of classical liberal entrepreneurs who favor the transformation of the Internet into the "ultimate market."[143] His old partner, Paul Allen, argues for the complete privatization of education. The world-spanning enterprise of the deregulation of telecommunications is clearly connected to the neo-liberal push in this area.

At this stage it is undoubtedly necessary to make a distinction between the classical liberal and the "capitalist-liberal" currents. As the economist Michel Gensollen notes,

> The industrial revolution of the end of the 18th century was triggered by two major innovations occasionally brought together under the vague term of classical liberalism: the classical liberal doctrine proper, and the great capitalist enterprise. [...] One reserves the term "classical liberalism" for the initial intuition of Mandeville, revisited by Smith, according to which it is useless to inculcate any moral rules of cooperation whatever or to develop complex regulations in order to assure the forward march of society; giving free rein to everyone's egoism and opportunism will, under certain con-

---

[143] Bill Gates, *The Road Ahead, op. cit.*, p. 6.

ditions, lead to the optimal situation or at least to a better situation than that obtained by the precise control of each one. [...] In fact, the great enterprises have always been in conflict with constraints which classical liberalism puts on their search for a dominant position to gain leverage in the competition.[144]

We should note in passing the many alliances between the large capitalist enterprises and national states—notably in the United States—at the heart of what has been called the military-industrial complex, in which the universities are implicated. IBM remains the symbol of this period. Informatics, the networks, or the Internet would not be so developed without the immense public investment in research and development. Bill Gates has built a huge capitalist empire that is currently [2000] embattled by anti-trust lawsuits—through classical-liberal-inspired legislation—and by the small businesses of the "net-economy" that wish to have options for development other than monopolistic concentration.[145]

The liberal-libertarian alliance

The increase in power of the Internet today favors the free-market absolutist thrust in this area, where one sees many small concerns set out to attack the large capitalist enterprises, competing with them in the "creation of value." It is not a matter of a simple economic competition between old and new businesses, but of two different spirits. The first favors accumulation and protection, the second consumption and openness. In the latter case, we are far from the influence of the rigorous Protestant monotheism analyzed by Max Weber and which was partly responsible for the birth of capital-

---

[144] Michel Gensollen, "La création de valeur sur Internet," *Réseaux*, no 97, CNET, 1999, p. 63-64.
[145] Solveig Godeluck, *Le boom de la netéconomie. Comment Internet bouleverse les règles du jeu économique,* La Découverte, Paris, 2000.

ism. The "new economy" is indeed supported by a new and different religiosity.

In the last few years the free-market pole has extended itself through the alliance which seemed to tie it to the libertarian counter-culture—this rapprochement does not, however, extend beyond this area, as is evident in the very symbolic agreement in France and in Europe between certain left-libertarians like Daniel Cohn-Bendit and free market absolutists like Alain Madelin. The fierce dedication to creating a world society without states, without borders, and without law finds in this its ideal goal.

Will the new religiosity surrounding a transparent and open world serve as a point of support for this alliance, an alliance that is not without historic consequence? It is certain that in return it would find an effective means for the diffusion of its beliefs. Pierre Lévy, that old anti-establishment militant (at least it should follow that he remain one), gives us the key to understanding this evolution in progress, which his point of view expresses and perfectly summarizes. According to him, "money will become a unit of epistemological measurement"[146] and "the economy will increasingly step up the ontological ladder toward the virtual, in the direction of that which creates existence."[147]

Thus, the connection is established by that author, between the information mystique and the search for profit, which constitutes a "measure." He does not hesitate to affirm, from such a perspective, that

> The more virtual one becomes, the more money one makes. The more one rises to the world of ideas, the more the market rewards. [...] There is no difference between thought and

---

[146] Pierre Lévy, *World philosophie, op. cit.*, p. 93.
[147] *Ibid.*, p. 134.

business. Money rewards the ideas that will bring the most fabulous future, the future which we decide to purchase.[148]

The information mystique has clearly espoused the market-libertarian current. The first targets at risk are the national states and the large capitalist enterprises.

The youthism of the new technologies

Our picture of the wide range of values and currents of thought upon which the cult of the Internet takes support for its diffusion would be incomplete without mentioning a value that is "secondary" with respect to the major ideological foundations we have mentioned: youthism, the tendency to exalt youth, their values, and to make of youth an obligatory model for all behavior. The cult of the Internet is a youth cult, of youth and for youth. It was born as a sort of process of "permanent revolution," where it is the "young" who determine the direction of the movement. Nicholas Negroponte is the author who goes the furthest in describing this youthism:

> I see the same decentralized mind-set growing in our society, driven by young citizenry in the digital world. The traditional centralist view of life will become a thing of the past. The nation-state itself is subject to tremendous change... While the politicians struggle with the baggage of history, a new generation is emerging from the digital landscape, free of many of the old prejudices. [...] Digital technology can be a natural force drawing people into greater world harmony.[149]

Negroponte underlines the role that youth have played in the establishment of a "counterculture to the establishment of computer science."

---

[148] *Ibid.*, p. 100.
[149] Nicholas Negroponte, *Being Digital, op. cit.*, p. 229-230.

[...] The common bond was not a discipline, but a belief that computers would dramatically alter and affect the quality of life through their ubiquity, not just in science, but in every aspect of living.[150]

He is one of many defenders of the idea that children "by nature" take to informatics:

Whether it is the demographics of the Internet, the use of Nintendo and Sega, or even the penetration of home computers, the dominant forces are not social or racial or economic but generational. The haves and the have-nots are now the young and the old.[151]

As one can see, youthism comes with a certain demagogy. It is in every case within the youngest layer of the population that the cult of information finds its support. Microsoft, currently seeking to negotiate changes that would bring it closer to the world of the Internet, does not hesitate to recruit the very young to direct its strategy. "The company," we are told, "estimates that these young people will almost constantly be on the Web. [...] The firm has therefore charged two teenagers with explaining to the middle aged directors their new philosophy of work and leisure."[152] One of them explained, "the periods of education, of work, of rest which used to seem distinct and successive are today mixed."[153]

It is in this framework of youthism that one finds the systematic defense of "speed," which has become a new belief: what is fast is better, closer to the world of the spirit. Speed is that which frees us from the body and brings us permanently closer to others. "The reality of information," says Paul Virilio, "is completely contained in the speed of its dissemina-

---

[150] *Ibid.*, p. 225

[151] *Ibid.*, p. 204

[152] *Le Monde*, 6 May 2000, p. 25.

[153] *Ibid.*, p. 25.

tion."[154] Commenting with conviction on the trial of José
Bové and his comrades, in July of 2000 in Millau, one of the
libertarian defenders of the Internet, Alain Madelin, claimed:

> In reality, the new world that is coming brings a formidable
> chance for the rebirth of a human-sized society, and in that
> new world, it is not the big that triumphs over the small, but
> the fast that wins against the slow.[155]

Reading certain articles and pronouncements, one could
well ask what place is left in the "new world" for the old
(those beyond 35). One study made by the *Caisse nationale
d'assurance vieillesse* showed a real discourse of exclusion regarding the aged in the area of new information technologies,[156] due primarily to the youthism on which this world is
based.

A technological utopia?

The cult of the Internet, as we have characterized it, presents certain traits in common with the technological utopias
that emerge with each great wave of technical innovation.
According to Howard Segal,[157] the United States, which has
put technology at the center of its culture, has seized upon it
as a utopia; but this time, contrary to the utopian traditions,
has in fact realized it—or believes that it has. (We have ourselves, in an earlier work, advanced an idea of the utopian

---

[154] Paul Virilio, *L'art du moteur, op. cit.*, p. 179. English translation: *The Art of
the Motor, op. cit.*, p. 140.

[155] "L'opposition contre la 'Bové Pride'," *Le Monde*, 2-3 juillet 2000, p. 6.

[156] Annie Bosquet and Philippe Breton, "La place des personnes âgées dans
l'argumentaire et le discours d'accompagnement des nouvelles technologies
de communication," *Rapport de recherche MIRE-CNAV*, mars 1998.

[157] Howard Segal, *Technological Utopianism in American Culture*, University of
Chicago Press, Chicago, 1985.

dimension of communication, beyond the technological dimension of informatics.[158])

In a very thorough article on the subject, in which he examined the results of the technological utopias since the 18th century, Armand Mattelart connects communication with the "promise of redemption." Already, Saint-Simonism, like the new ideology of the network, had come under the influence of religiosity. The engineer was at the origin of a whole new Church.[159]

The nineteenth century was not lacking in prophets, engineers, revolutionaries or sociologists to nourish what Philippe Chanial calls the "paradigm of the matrix of the Association," inseparable, according to him, "from a reference to the religious, itself metaphorical." Religion (*religio, religare*) is, the author adds,

> [...] synonymous with the social bond, of unity, of convergence. Thus the religious designates less a mystical need than the necessary bond of the community. The Association, by reestablishing these bonds, realizes the true religion.[160]

Armand Mattelart recalls that the anarchist utopia of Peter Kropotkin made electricity the point of departure for a new society. But is every project for society a utopia? The religion which promises an afterlife, is it too a utopia? The term suffers, as Lucien Sfez also recognizes, from imprecision.[161] If utopia implies simply a desire to "leave the world," a radical rupture with all aspects of the old world, then the new religiosity that is formed from the Internet is partial relief. Yet it is

---

[158] Philippe Breton, *L'utopie de la communication, op. cit.*

[159] On this subject see also Pierre Musso, *Télécommunicatins et philosophie des réseaux, op. cit.*

[160] Philippe Chanial, "Le projet utopique des sciences sociales: le paradigme de l'association," *Quaderni*, op. cit., p. 81.

[161] Lucien Sfez, introduction to *Quaderni* no 40, 1999-2000, op. cit.

indeed more than that. It is a cosmic vision of the world—far from the narrowness of islands and utopian cities, even those made of glass. As Gianni Vattimo suggests, it is more a question of a "heterotopie,"[162] in a new world that no longer has a center.

There is no doubt, in any case, that the new cult is supported by the "desire for utopia," a perhaps more concrete category which designates that desire for a psychological and political break that animates many of our contemporaries. That desire for utopia serves as the basis for accepting the most radical proposals for building a "new world" where consciousnesses will regroup in the heart of a collective global network.

Utopia, like religion, always implies a profound change of the "social bond," that is to say of the manner in which human beings live together. It is unquestionably on this precise point that the new faith is the most concrete and the most active. The cult of the Internet implies a new way of life that must be imposed on all, believers and non-believers alike.

---

[162] Gianni Vattimo, *La société transparente*, op. cit., p. 83. English ed.: *The Transparent Society, op. cit.*

6.

The taboo against direct encounter

One question today evokes much resistance at the same time as it fascinates many of our contemporaries in a very ambivalent manner: the question of direct encounter and its symmetrical opposite, the question of separation. For the first time in human history, under the influence of the new religious faith in information, transparence, and the reunification of consciousness, we have made a communications network capable, if it is pushed to its limits, of separating human beings and of enabling them to dispense with all direct human encounter.

The most radical partisans of the Internet always take the same line: in order to be able to benefit from all the promises that the new communication networks hold, in order to reach the "new world" in which the human being will finally be fully realized—or better, superseded—it is necessary to transfer to the Internet the majority of all those activities which have until now been pursued otherwise: work, leisure, television, cinema, commerce, relations with others, prayer, thinking, and for the extremists, sex.

In practice, all the beliefs of the new faith converge towards a unique point: all communication, all relations, all encounters must pass through the network. The content of the "old world" must be reversed within the "new world" by leaving behind everything that is opposed to the rise of the collective consciousness.

The question of violence

Is the simple promise of a better world enough to justify such a radical change of the social bond? If we stop the enquiry here, it would lack a fundamental dimension, which is sketched out in all that we are about to describe. Does the desire for a better world not correspond as well to the vivid perception that our current world is marked by the red-hot brand of violence?

We have seen that cyberspace as a world of light and transparence embodies the utopia of peace. There, violence is identified and rejected along with the body, animality, materiality. The price of peace is a double separation, on the one hand, of the body from the spirit, and on the other hand, of bodies from each other.

There we are at the heart of a conception probably arising from North American culture, from its particular relation to violence. In a passionate analysis of violence in the United States, sociologist Denis Duclos notes what he feels is the "great intuition of Anglo-American culture: civilization is precarious. The more it occupies the immense area with its 'system,' its networks, its markets, its technology, the more civilization appears as a fine tissue on the surface of savage reality. One moment of inattention and the bubble bursts, the most sophisticated Harvard diplomat returns to a state of a carnivorous brute."[163]

He adds, "the spectacle of violence rarely opens up a civilizing process in the United States but normally a hesitation, an oscillation between savagery and civility, between peace and aggression."[164] In that spirit, the Internet could well be a hopeless attempt to escape from that permanent oscillation. While undergoing a revival in the United States, especially

---

[163] Denis Duclos, *Le complexe du loup-garou,* op. cit., p. 52.
[164] *Ibid.,* p. 25.

under the influence of Buddhism and Zen philosophy, religious values well beyond the world of the Internet, but clearly connected to it, created not only a large space for the identification of violence and Evil, including conflict in its many forms, but also an ideal of peace and non-violence.

From this point of view one finds a clear cultural difference with Europe. European cultures are also concerned to make an end to destructive violence, but they are also attached to agonistic concepts (which privilege dynamic opposition) of the social bond, of discussion, and of social relations.

In this sense, the aspiration toward peace of social relations, which is one of the promises, perhaps the major promise of the cult of the Internet, especially resonates with a typically American cultural dimension. Therefore, in this new conception of the social bond, are Evil and violence not embodied by the Other, by the direct encounter with the Other and the necessity of dividing the territory with that Other, of the necessity of "breathing the same air"? One notes also the convergence with hygienics, an American value at least since the twenties.

This implies that one should keep the Other at a distance since the Other is the carrier of the aggressive "germs" of all of nature. In such a context, as David Le Breton writes,

> The denigration of the body [...] in the radical discourse of certain scientists or members of cyberculture, is also a real fact for millions of Westerners who have lost any clear relation to a body which they use only partially.[165]

The cult of the Internet proposes nothing less than taking that avenue of escape to the extreme, to enclose each individual in his bubble as the price of finally obtaining peaceful universal communion. All the advantages of communication

---

[165] David Le Breton, *L'adieu au corps, op. cit.*, p. 15.

without its risks—this is perhaps the main promise of the new cult, one of the most active underground reasons for its current success. The Internet finally brings peace to a troubled world, which can see no other way to make peace...

The alternative to chaos

That question already haunted Norbert Wiener. The founder of cybernetics saw violence as the height of entropy:

> For this random element, this organic incompleteness, is one which without too violent a figure of speech we may consider evil; the negative evil which St. Augustine characterizes as incompleteness, rather than the positive malicious evil of the Manichaeans.[166]

In his extremely pessimistic vision of the future (the reverse of the current believers, so confident in the future), he saw the universe sliding irresistibly toward the chaos of entropy, as "the universe as a whole... tends to run down."[167] Pierre Lévy inherits part of that cybernetic vision, when he affirms that "the world [...] is always on the edge of chaos and disorganization [and that] the species is not yet completely civilized."[168]

In this view, the growth of all the "cyber-technologies" corresponds well to the hope of a receding of violence. One finds there a belief now largely shared, in spite of the fragility of its foundation: information, communication, reduces evil. As Jacques Bureau said in an old work that was a plea for the arrival of a "logical era,"

> The riot [...] was for a long time the only weapon for man alone. But if information freely circulates, man is not alone: he is integrated in a global system of interpretation and logi-

---

[166] Norbert Wiener, *The Human use of Human Beings*, 1954 op cit., p. 11
[167] *Ibid.*, p. 12
[168] Pierre Lévy, *World philosophie, op. cit.*, p. 12.

cal management of all matters, linking him with all the others; together they form a true society."[169]

The ideal world, the true society, is truly that transparent "noosphere" that "will save us from catastrophes, from the danger of injustice, from ecological disequilibrium."[170]

Yet there is a price to pay in order for the core of the promise—the eradication of all violence—to be realized. And that price is precisely social separation, the end of all direct encounter.

A prudent strategy

It is true that not everyone subscribes to such extreme views. Many enthusiastic defenders of the Internet can say: "We have never held such ideas! We have never advocated the end of physical encounter, for example!" We shall look further at that later on.

Here it is necessary to distinguish between the "partisans of rational use" who see in the Internet a communications tool complementing other tools, and the radicals, members of the new cult, for whom the absorption of humanity in the network has become a goal. For these latter, it is not so much the network that counts as its ability to privilege blessed information. For them, the Internet is a Church that permits those who so desire to consecrate themselves wholly to communication and communion.

That distinction is not always easy to make. Those who have a reasonable, "lay" point of view concerning the new information technologies are sometimes susceptible to the siren's song of the prophets. They always listen to these latter with attention and interest even if they do not share their radical ideas. The music of their ideas resonates in the imagi-

---

[169] Jacques Bureau, *L'ère logique, op. cit.*, p. 13.
[170] Pierre Lévy, *World philosophie, op. cit.*, p. 174.

nation and gives it meaning. They are thinking "It is true, they exaggerate a bit, but in the end..." The lyrical flight of a Philippe Quéau on "cyberspace," on the Internet which "will endow every organ of our bodies with an email address"[171] permitting them to live autonomously on the network, gives an ambivalent joy to those who desire that their most concrete and down to earth activities be "spiritually" uplifted in some manner.

This distinction is also difficult to maintain because the most excited militants of the cult of the Internet, when they are confronted with reality, do not hesitate to use a very old strategy of persuasion. In the seventies, the partisans of the "information revolution," ancestors of today's militants, took this strategy to get around "the users resistance to change." They proceeded along two paths: the first approach was a matter of affirming that all these machines were "nothing but tools" which did not alter their ends at all. Then, once the tools were in place, they, especially the most ardent converts, dazzled all with the suggestion that they were at the heart of a real revolution, that they had, thanks to technology, "to change the world." Everything new that is put forth raises hesitations and reservations; the first strategic move responds: "It is only a tool..." We see the same thing today.

Everyone knows well that by dint of proposing to mediate everything *via* a network that does everything, this question of the separation of bodies is going to be posed first. So our most militant authors take up a prudent attitude to this subject, which, for good reasons, is not without contradictions. On the one hand, they insist that the network must absorb all our activities (that is the true stake, the true spiritual revolution); on the other, they guarantee us, to be sure, physical

---

[171] Remarks by Philippe Quéau at the colloquium *"De Gutenberg ao terceiro milénio," loc. cit.*

encounters will not only not be eliminated but that they will even be...augmented!

Thus, after having forcefully affirmed that humanity is "on the way to recollecting itself in an immense virtual village, where one has more choices, where one can meet with the whole world, where better markets are found, including and above all markets for information, knowledge, relationships and entertainment,"[172] and that "web sites are like boutiques, offices and mansions; the discussion groups and the virtual communities ... are like places, cafes, salons, of elective associations," and finally "the interactive virtual worlds, more or less playful, are the new works of art, the cinemas, theaters, and operas of the 21st century," Pierre Lévy adds, as if to calm the questions that might arise from that radical assertion that to which we should do everything always at a distance: "Still we continue to physically move ourselves, to meet each other in the flesh, probably more than now, since the phenomena of relation and interconnection of all sorts (virtual or not) will be amplified and accelerated."[173]

It is hard to see how there could still be a place for direct encounter in the heart of a thought that systematically exalts the virtual encounter. Nor is it possible to see, once all the activities previously presupposing direct encounter have been "virtualized," what really remains as a practical possibility from that point of view... Once you have everything done *via* the network, in the areas that have been described, then what is left to do in an eventual direct encounter?

Similarly, for the former guru of the sixties, Timothy Leary, converted preacher of cyberspace, who, after having affirmed that "in a very near future we will be implicated in a number of cyber-relations with people whom we shall undoubtedly never meet in person, [...] all that without leaving

[172] Pierre Lévy, *World philosophie, op. cit.*, p. 60.
[173] *Ibid.*, p. 58.

our room," adds, as if to pass over the radicalism of his proposal, that "the direct exchanges, face to face, will be reserved for great occasions."[174] Yet this last remark was written from that point of view in which everything has been done to eliminate direct encounter, which is subject, in the words of the author, to the "slavery of the body."[175] As we shall see, of the many texts coming out of the "cyberculture," hardly any take precautions and declare outright that the great interest of the Internet is exactly that it dispenses with direct encounter and all of its "inconveniences."

In a general way, even for those who do not insist on this latter dimension, many projects linked to the Internet are oriented toward the possibility of not having to leave home. In a study on that subject, the journalist Stéphane Mandard described the ideal future house being built near Brussels:

> Everything is made so that one feels good there. [...] The garden grows by itself. [...] The dichotomy work/home is a thing of the past, in the networked house one works at home. Appointments are managed from a distance, meetings take place by videoconference, research reports arrive by electronic courier, information is found on the Web. [...] Education henceforth takes place in the digital realm: online courses and tutors have definitely relegated in-person teaching—i.e. classroom instruction—to the man in the moon."[176]

Likewise, the public's attention has recently been drawn to a new side of the "ability to do it at home": prayer, confession, and even the spiritual retreat on the Internet.[177]

---

[174] Cited in David Le Breton, *L'adieu au corps, op. cit.*
[175] *Ibid.*
[176] Stéphane Mandard, "La vie rêvée des domoticiens," *Le Monde interactif*, 2 février 2000.
[177] Xavier Ternisien, "Les religions sont entrées en force sur Internet," *Le Monde* 9-10 juillet 2000.

Is not the promise that physical encounter "will be augmented" a matter of rhetorical tactic in view of the anticipated reality which everyone presents as systematically putting up obstacles to encounter? In fact, the partisans of "Internet-for-everything" cannot very well understand why one would want to do directly what can be done on the network! These are the stakes. The common affirmation, repeated and recurrent in this milieu, is that *in order to realize the promise, we must separate.* That is the price to pay.

A description of the "Global information society"

Science fiction furnishes numerous examples of this project for a new social bond. These illustrations have in return nourished the imagination of the partisans of the cult of the Internet. The stories are parables that allow the further spread of the good news. Thus science fiction plays a great role in the development of the new faith.

For the reader, the pertinence of a science fiction narrative, of a description, lies in its realism, that is to say, in its capacity to anticipate what will actually occur. Far from being fiction, it is a guide for action. (According to some studies, it is the most widely read genre among computer professionals).[178] Many works set forth the future information society. For the most part, from Isaac Asimov and Philip K. Dick through William Gibson, J.G. Ballard and Jean-Michel Truong, their descriptions of that society are oriented around the question of the social bond, and at their center they evoke the social separation that is the pivot of these new worlds.

The authors of most of these works go straight to the point: it is indeed the question of violence that is posed at the center of the problematic of the new society, whether it is a

---

[178] Philippe Breton, "L'informaticien et la sécurité: enquête sur un antagonisme," *loc. cit.*

matter of the fear of epidemics or more fundamentally of the fear of the presence of the Other as a source of violence. In every case, the Internet represents the end of the unbearable tension provoked by the Other.

The fear of epidemics

Jean-Michel Truong furnishes a very imaginative illustration,[179] evocative and powerful, in his description of a world where, following the threat of epidemic—real or feared—the majority of humanity submits to a "great closing up." Each individual finds himself once again alone in an apartment from which it is impossible to leave. These steel boxes are piled one on top of the other to form giant pyramids all linked together by the Internet. Communication is constant but entirely virtual.

The world is divided into three classes: the "no-plugs," clandestinely living in packs, submitting themselves to a hostile nature; those who live separated one from another; and a small class of the wealthy who have the right to meet each other and live in a universe protected from all external aggression.

The violence of the Other

A rather terrifying novel by J.G. Ballard portrays a world where humans can communicate only by means of images and never meet each other:

> At that time neither I nor anyone else had ever dreamed that we might actually meet in person. In fact, age-old though

---

[179] Jean-Michel Truong, *Le successeur de Pierre, op. cit.*

rarely invoked ordinances still existed to prevent this—to meet another human being was an indictable offence.[180]

The reason for that absence of direct connection we find only in the story's denouement: resolved to meet, a man, a woman and their children end by shooting each other in homicidal furor.

Incidentally, the prohibition of incest is evoked as one of the motifs of that separation; but, more widely, direct encounter with the Other cannot but provoke deception, frustration, and an increase of irrepressible violence. Virtual communication has the immense advantage of eliminating that dimension of human relations, thereby pacifying us. The author thus relates the amorous encounter of his characters: "We began to go out together—that is we shared the same films on television, visited the same theatres and concert halls, watched the same meals prepared in restaurants, all within the comfort of our respective homes."[181] Marriage for them is also at a distance, and the honeymoon consists of them watching "together," i.e. "simultaneously," films about Venice...

Here we indeed find a number of today's actual themes. As if in echo, Bill Gates, with great naiveté, tells us of one of his relations "at a distance":

I used to date a woman who lived in a different city. We spent a lot of time together on e-mail. And we figured out a way we could sort of go to the movies together. We'd find a film that was playing at about the same time in both our cities. We'd drive to our respective theaters, chatting on our cellular phones. We'd watch the movie, and on the way home we'd use our cell phones again to discuss the show. In the future this sort of "virtual dating" will be better because

[180] J.G. Ballard, "The intensive care unit" in *Myths of the Near Future*, Jonathan Cape, London, 1982.
[181] *Ibid.*, p. 200.

the movie watching could be combined with a videoconference.[182]

A very jarring short film by the American director Hal Salwen, which unfortunately went almost unseen, *Denise on the Telephone* (1996) portrays people who live alone but constantly keep in touch in the most intimate fashion, by telephone. The attempt by two of the protagonists to meet in person turns out badly. The violence of the direct meeting is too strong for these two who are accustomed to continuous virtual communication.

For the promoters of the cult of the Internet, it is evidently not a matter of a simple desire for "separation." We have seen how many among them insist, above all, on the "reunification of consciousness." The new social bond is doubly and irreducibly characterized by a separation (of individuals) and a communion (of spirits), as the condition for social peace. This movement, for Pierre Lévy, following Teilhard de Chardin, is in progress:

> Just before its reunification the collective consciousness had hesitated. Would it remain divided, at war with itself? These were the great world wars and the cold war. And then one day, sometime during the nineties of the 20th century, it decided that it would be better to stop fighting itself and form a single collective consciousness, a single fortress of light. To be sure there still remain "nations," "cultural identities," civil wars and dictators. But they are fewer and fewer; they are nothing but signs of cultural backwardness. In a few decades, a century at the most, they will all have disappeared.[183]

The themes of physical separation and virtual communication as conditions of a better world, or on the other hand, for some authors, of "bettering worlds" to paraphrase Aldous

---

[182] Bill Gates, *The Road Ahead, op. cit.,* p. 206.
[183] Pierre Lévy, *World philosophie, op. cit.,* p. 46-47.

Huxley, is indeed the imaginative matrix which serves as the thought of the world of the Internet.

The solar society of Asimov

The first "visualization" of a society in which a complete communication network (sound and image) occupies a determining place in social life replacing all traditional collective order goes back to the American popularizer of science, Isaac Asimov, and his proposal of 1955.[184] We shall dwell for a moment on the particulars of communication in such a world.

Since the 1940s, this prolific author has devoted an important part of his career to promoting the importance of "communication machines," while at the same time investigating the consequences of what was at that time still called "robotics" (not only in the industrial sense but in the more general sense of systematically putting computers and "artificial intelligences" to work). He was responsible for the "Three Laws of Robotics," intended to establish the ethical boundaries for the development of these machines.

We also note, since it is not without importance, that the only true communication "network" of information which existed at that time was a project vast in size (the equivalent of the Manhattan Project for informatics), but totally unknown to the public, since it was a very strictly classified "military secret": the American air defense network SAGE,[185] which would be the ancestor of the Internet network.

The information society that Asimov described strictly followed the cybernetic discourse of the times, and was understood to be an imaginary world, situated on a planet far from Earth, "Solaria." The communication system that is at

---

[184] Isaac Asimov, *Naked Sun. op. cit.*
[185] Philippe Breton, *Histoire de l'informatique, op. cit.*

the center of social life in that world described by Asimov was a very precise anticipation of the Internet. The technologies of communication described in the text are of little importance for the comparison—he writes of robots which serve as intermediaries of communication—but the function described is similar.

At every point of access to the network—and they are everywhere—one can have access to the Others. The network transports images and sound. The audiovisual devices, true ancestors of multimedia as we know it, allow access to knowledge. The images are "virtual." (Asimov called it "stereovision.")[186] The description of technical devices is accompanied by a description of the particular social bond that they entail. This is characterized foremost by a taboo central to the imaginary world described here, that of the direct encounter. The men and women who populate that world live alone from infancy to death surrounded by much property and many robots, all in continuous communication with the other inhabitants *via* the network. We shall examine here some excerpts from the book that give these descriptions, and see how the question of a new social bond is put.

A world without encounter

Asimov first describes that possibility offered to the inhabitants of Solaria: constant communication everywhere. He gives few technical details about the means utilized other than that they pass through anthropomorphic machines. This is the sole real difference from current networks, since the anthropomorphic reference in the equivalent technological forms have disappeared for the time being:

---

[186] In the original English version of Asimov's book the distinction is between "seeing" (direct encounter) and "viewing" (mediated encounter). The French version translates "viewing" as "stereovision"—tr.

From this house, partner Elijah [the character Elijah is used to explain to us how the planet on which the stranger finds himself functions] you can obtain a three-dimensional view of anyone on the planet. There will be no problem. In fact, it will save you the annoyance of leaving this house.[187]

The planet Solaria is entirely knit together by this communication network, and when one wishes to "meet" someone, the room in which they sit is divided in two and the image of the other appears virtually. (Asimov does not use this latter term). The network reproduces the decor and makes a three-dimensional figure of the person with whom they are in contact. Thus one can "eat" with someone very far away:

You're viewing me right now. You can't touch me, can you, or smell me, or anything like that. You could if you were seeing me. Right now, I'm two hundred miles away from you at *least*. So how can it be the same thing? [...] No, you don't see me. You see my image. You're viewing me.[188]

The whole question lies in that difference between direct and indirect presence. The organization of the social bond turns on that question. Society consists neither of towns, each person living alone in a property separated from the others, nor of States. The demographic characteristics of that planet are rather special: the number of inhabitants remains constant, eugenics is the rule, and, in the world described by Asimov, one grows old but never truly ages. (Neither body nor mind deteriorate). Thus, each one, no matter his age, remains in complete possession of his physical and mental capacities.

The necessity of physical separation

---

[187] Isaac Asimov, *Naked Sun, op. cit.* p. 40-41.
[188] *Ibid.,* p. 49.

The central taboo, the organizer of the social bond in that world, is the physical encounter: "Well, you saw one another often?" the stranger to Solaria asks. "What? I should hope not. We're not animals, you know."[189] This point is essential. Physical encounter is identified with animality, brutality and violence. It is this taboo and the respect for it that allows the members of this society to define the character of their relations as "civilized."

This taboo is very well accepted, since not only the means of communication permit the complete avoidance of all encounters, but should an accidental meeting occur, it would be physically intolerable: "We spoke a few minutes; seeing *is* an ordeal;"[190]

> "I thought I was enduring personal presence so well, but that was a delusion. I was quite on edge, and your phrase pushed me over it, in a manner of speaking. [...] The phrase conjured up the most striking picture of the two of us breathing—breathing one another's breath." The Solarian shuddered. "Don't you find that repulsive?"[191]

At one stroke, sex is shifted to animality. (Infants are born thanks to technologies of artificial procreation). There is therefore nothing wrong, no breaking of the taboo, in appearing nude by virtual image before others: "It is only viewing, you see," Gladia says after having appeared in the nude.[192] Even the doctors practice "telemedicine" before its time.

In that society, the final obstacle to the most complete possible physical separation between the people who make up that society is the education of children, which, at the be-

---

[189] *Ibid.*, p. 103.
[190] *Ibid.*, p. 51-52.
[191] *Ibid.*, p. 107
[192] *Ibid.*, p. 48.

ginning, must still be done in groups. But that question is in the process of being settled:

> Those fetuses back there have gills and a tail for a time. Can't skip those steps. The youngster has to go through the social-animal stage in the same way. But just as a fetus can get through in one month a stage that evolution took a hundred million years to get through, so our children can hurry through the social-animal stage. Dr. Delmarre was of the opinion that with the generations, we'd get through that stage faster and faster [...] In three thousand years, he estimated, at the present rate of progress, we'd have children who'd take to viewing at once.[193]

A new inaptitude for direct communication?

The systematic practice of communication through the intermediary of computers and networks is the actual reality of the new cult of the Internet. We can now better understand a number of practices suggested by the internauts, which all turn up the same imperative: communicate, all the time, always, as much as possible, no matter the content! Activate information: here is the true rite to which one makes sacrifice every hour of the day and of the night.

Will the price of the apparent ease in mediated communication be the development of an inaptitude for direct confrontation? Will the cult of the Internet imply just this sacrifice? In the universe of "Internet-for-everything," the individual is led to make use of his own territory of personal evolution, at the heart of which he will no longer have anything whatever to do with other people. Each one becomes in some way sovereign over his own territory and finds no more interest in finding himself sovereign over that of the Other.

In the allegory set forth by Asimov, the areas in which both the one and the other live are situated in the country—if

---

[193] *Ibid.,* p. 130

that expression still makes any sense in a world without towns. Their borders are secure and unbreakable. "Breathing one another's breath" becomes completely unbearable. This is indeed the ideal of Bill Gates who argues for such a life "in the country."

The expected progress in the area of mobile telecommunications, especially in conjunction with the Internet, will not be an obstacle to such separation. One can very well be alone in the midst of a crowd. Isolation here is provoked not by geography but by technological instruments that separate individuals. Paul Virilio said "portable virtual environments"[194] could well come to pass. In a certain sense, such a "society" becomes a global society, not because exchanges take place in the same "global village," but because each one becomes a world unto himself. This is, perhaps, the most appropriate meaning that should be given today to the notion of "globalization."

---

[194] Paul Virilio, *L'art du moteur, op. cit.*, p. 183. English ed.: *The Art of the Motor, op. cit.*, p. 145.

7.

A threat to the social bond?

Looking at the whole picture, what have we found so far? The talk among the most active Internet enthusiasts is marked, indeed determined, by a diffuse religiosity that gives it its true dynamic. This religiosity appears as non-deist, spiritualist, dualist and anti-humanist. It extols the unification of consciousnesses, bringing together human beings and "intelligent machines" in a single continuum. It supposes a movement of history from matter to spirit, from the reunion of consciousnesses to their absorption in a global unification. The essential practices of this new religiosity are constant communication, physical separation and the end of direct encounter, a rejection of law and mediation, and confusion between the representation and the represented, between the virtual and the real.

Does this faith have a future or is it nothing more than the froth that accompanies the always-enthusiastic beginning of a new technological paradigm? Will the Internet of tomorrow be as invisible—and as indispensable—as electricity, which no one today sees as the basis of a new spirituality? Or on the contrary, are we on the verge of that "metamorphosis of God" that will lead the 21st century toward new spiritualities by associating them with science and above all with technology? Are we, as Henri Tincq asks, entering an era of "transcendence without God"? In these conditions, he states, "the religious word becomes suspect, but spirituality is in fashion."[195] If this is to be the case, will it not be necessary to again pose the question of secularism in the modern world, and to renew that problematic as well? Should we not have the choice of separating the Internet from the cult of which it is the object?

Two models of Internet development

The actual development of the Internet can be analyzed as the fruit of a contradictory tension between two models: the strategy of Internet-for-everything, which is the matrix of that new religiosity, and the more pragmatic approach of all those who see in the Internet a valuable tool, but only a tool. It is difficult to evaluate the respective influences of these two models. Here we shall make the hypothesis that at the dawn of the 21st century the Internet-for-everything strategy is the most attractive, and exercises a real fascination, especially over the young. Many young people in fact see in the Internet the possibility of realizing the transformation of society into one that fits their desires. The new religiosity fills the same role as the utopian revolutionaries of the sixties and seventies. (We have already seen the continuity of influences from this point of view.) It captivates the desire for change, bringing it out of the political sphere.

We have also established that one of the reasons for the success of the new religiosity is its convergence with the values of the market economy. In so far as the option "Internet-for-everything" will correspond to the terrain of the opening of new markets and the perspective of new sources of profit in the world of stockholders, the current dominant model of Internet development will continue. This does not exclude the possibility that certain irreversible transformations linked

---

[195] Henri Tincq, "La métamorphose de Dieu," supplement to *Le Monde/L'Avenir*, 2000-2099.

to the growing use of the Internet will not one day prevent the partisans of the new cult from an alliance with free market ideas, found embarrassing by those who are nearer to a tradition which is indifferent and even hostile to the materiality of money and consumption.

On this point it is tempting to make an analogy with Buddhism. That doctrine is attractive for many since in a first stage of practice it focuses the attention on the body and the spirit. Its success owes much to the modern attraction to certain hedonistic bodily practices and to meditation. But the following stage is indeed different, since it is truly a matter of passing beyond that attraction through a perspective of emptiness, of denial of the body and of thought.

The legitimacy of the dominant model of Internet development is built upon the promises it makes. It is this, rather than the diffusion of beliefs—which in the end is an individual matter—that constitutes the grounds of the argument for the Internet-for-everything option offered to the public. The public had little access to the religious designs behind the whole affair. In other words, we have something that unfolds in two stages, where the promises of a better world and of a better existence allow the progressive attraction of people to a new vision of the world. As is already said in certain religious groups: first do it; you will understand later.

These promises and the reconstruction of the social bond that accompanies them as a condition are, however, susceptible to many questions, even if the conditions of the debate on the subject are unfavorable to a clear evaluation of what is at stake. Will these promises really be fulfilled? Is there not, in the rapid development of new communication technologies, a double—and terrible—risk of solitude and of the collectivization of our thinking? Are the symbolic foundations of our culture not threatened while there is nothing to replace them? In sum, In sum, does not the Internet-for-everything option, before it even approaches the hypothetical new world, risk negative, even perverse effects? That is what some fear. Before hearing their arguments it is necessary to take stock of the conditions of the debate on these questions.

Information bordering on propaganda

To begin, we recall that the discussion must leave the false debate, "for or against the Internet," behind, and aim instead at the different models of development of that new technology. The "religious" approach that leads to making the "Internet-for-everything" argument is after all no more than one model of development among others, and it is legitimate as long as it remains open for discussion.

When one examines the manner in which the non-specialists, that is to say the vast majority, are informed, it appears that they are informed in a unilateral fashion. Three remarks on this: First, although discussions of the Internet are bathed in a diffuse religiosity full of promises, the true motives of the new cult are rarely explicit; next, the growing place accorded to the Internet is often presented as "ineluctable"; and finally, the new technologies are presented to us from a "deterministic" standpoint (the information networks will automatically change our way of life deeply and for the better). There appears to be practically no society-wide debate on these questions. This is undoubtedly because there is not, as in the case of nuclear power or genetically modified organisms, an awareness of an immediate threat. The social bond is a fact more abstract than food or the environment.

A quasi-clandestine approach

There are without doubt many reasons for the fact that this religiosity and the radical proposals for the transformation of social relationships that it implies are not better known to the larger public. One of these has to do with the fact that the explicitly anti-humanist point of view of these new conceptions is offensive to public opinion. The idea that man is the center of the world and must be the first source of our preoccupations concerning human beings is strongly implanted in the heart of many cultures. Any proposition that goes against this sense immediately elicits reserve and hostility.

From this point of view, the experience of cybernetics in the forties is interesting. Authors on cybernetics of that period had to stop popularizing their ideas, for example on the ontological difference between men and machines. The sanction has been very strong; the "cybernetic age" was rapidly discredited and has become practically buried. The resistance of the humanism that nourished our culture is very strong in spite of everything.

Authors writing today, besides those writing science fiction, are confronted with real difficulties in defending a similar point of view. One can note here, without making a strict comparison, on the one hand, the lively debates (this is a euphemism) elicited by the German philosopher Peter Sloterdijk when he defended the classic theses of the old cybernetics by explaining, for example, that "there is no more than that final metaphysical difference separating the organism from the machine, whether it is born or made, that still resists the rise of the thought of the post-metaphysical continuum,"[196] and, on the other hand, the difficult reception of Pierre Lévy's above-mentioned work *World philosophie*, especially in France.

The idea that machines can become intelligent has indeed been revived in the media recently, but it rarely goes beyond being merely a scientific curiosity or exotic utopia. Much of the resistance stirred up by the Internet is linked to the awareness that something has come into play that can be turned against man. The problem is clearly that this resistance

---

[196] Peter Sloterdijk, "Le centrisme mou au risque de penser," *loc. cit.*

throws the baby out with the bathwater, the good technologies with the global project associated with them.

From this fact, the new religiosity advances partly hidden by its explicit content, strongly influencing everything at the "intermediary" level, most of the message being the promotion of the Internet. This is particularly true for advertising, which is never content merely to inform us about the functionalities of the products being sold and often tries to build up their legitimacy. Thus, for many people, the Internet is associated with a whole group of values—such as universality, community, liberty, knowledge—without their being able to make any strong connections among them, and reinforcing the faith which is the idea behind it. Each transformation of a social activity into an activity taking place on the network, such as, for example, electronic commerce, is generally evaluated in isolation. Each stage of the "Internetization" of the world is in itself fascinating but insignificant. It is only when these factors are considered together that the problem becomes evident. The public finds itself asked to practice this new cult little by little, without being made to see all the consequences.

A form of proselytizing

Whence the sometimes propagandistic and proselytizing aspect of the operation: systematically pounding the implicit messages, repeated to saturation and provoking the acceptance of values solely through their enunciation, everything masking the most profound consequences of that acceptance.[197] "How much longer," Lucien Sfez asks, "must we still submit to the propaganda (if the word is not too weak) of the press and the government in favor of the Internet, eighth

---

[197] On the method of analyzing this type of manipulative technique, see Philippe Breton, *La parole manipulée*, La Découverte, Paris, 1998.

wonder of the world, without which there is no point in being healthy?"[198] It would certainly be too strong to speak about this as a sectarian mechanism, but some traits of the cult of the Internet are not far from being just that.

The arrival of digital technologies is the occasion of an immense uproar that reverberates everywhere: on television, in the media, in advertising, and in political speech as well as in everyday conversation. "I must get on with it," one often hears in a group of people who give more an impression of giving in to social pressure than expressing a real need. "I don't want to miss out on the action" is often added in the guise of an argument (to convince oneself).

Beyond a certain threshold of diffusion, a technology becomes indispensable, even if it is unwanted and its use causes problems. In 2000, it is difficult for many to do without the computer, email or cell phone; one cannot do without them except under pain of social isolation for recalcitrants and those minorities who propose alternative solutions. It is to reach that threshold that advertising aims first at the strata most sensitive to all the new forms of propaganda: youth, the privileged target of the promise of a new world.

The recent [2000] infatuation with the "net-economy" has shown the power of this discourse. The massive waves of stock buying of companies linked to the Internet are a matter of nothing other than speculators avid for immediate profits. The propaganda in favor of Internet-for-everything has attracted to the stock exchange even those for whom all this is new, and who have even borrowed money for the occasion. In the same way that one must connect to the Internet, it is necessary to participate in its economic sector and echo the promise. Money here is indeed a measure of the new world announced by the new information technologies. But it is essentially a matter of speculative money, in an economy that

---

[198] Lucien Sfez, preface to *Quaderni* no 40, 1999-2000, op. cit., p. 7.

constantly borders on a market crash.[199] When the velocity of money imitates the velocity of information it acquires a dangerous volatility.

As an emblematic illustration of that power of the discourse surrounding the Internet we should remember the ad campaign conducted at the beginning of the year 2000 by France Télécom, which led to an irrational increase in the value of its stock. At the end of that campaign, and in a single day, Thursday, the second of March, the stock value of the company increased more than 25% to 295 billion francs (45.6 million euros). That campaign had begun with a massive wave of advertising, the text of which should be no surprise since it has the same theme to the nth degree.

For example, in a full-page ad (the last page) of the daily newspaper *Le Monde*, one could read: "Today with France Télécom the life of each one is richer in interactions and possibilities. A new life has begun." The ad thus revived the new slogan inaugurated by France Télécom the 29th of February 2000, "Welcome to Life.com." Likewise, the chief executive officer, Michel Bon, multiplied the effects of the announcement, without any concrete promises, except the later orientation of society toward activity on the Internet. The general context in which that operation could succeed shows well the importance of the word and the promise. As the journalist Enguérand Renault said in an article commenting on the affair: "As to 'progress,' words counted for more than facts."[200] It could not be said better.

Will the Internet revolution continue?

The theme of the "ineluctability" of the "Internet revolution" is partially integrated with the advertising language that

---

[199] On these matters, one may profitably consult the work of Solveig Godeluck, *Le boom de la netéconomie, op. cit.*

[200] Enguérand Renault, *Le Monde*, 4 mars 2000, p. 23.

has invaded the media at the end of the nineties. It announces a revolution in way-of-life and of society itself that nothing can stop. The message is clear and devastating from the democratic point of view: Henceforth we no longer have any say in the major changes that are supposed to affect us!

The framework of the discourse on the information society is a deterministic argument. The Canadian academic Marshall McLuhan has played a large role in the conception and diffusion of that commonplace idea in the field of communication studies. As Dominique Wolton explains,

> These technological visions of the future are all founded on the idea, dominant in the United States, of the primacy of technology over society. Their greatest failure is ignorance of history [...] Blinded by technology, they do not know that human societies are always more complex than the most sophisticated technologies.[201]

The determinist hypothesis is too self-serving on the part of those who base their reasoning on it to be a true working hypothesis. That does not keep it from being extremely widespread, to the point of becoming a true commonplace that largely conditions our vision of the "impact of the new information technologies on society."

The ineluctability of the "Internet revolution" is supported by another hypothesis that ultimately reveals itself to be rather weak: the one that postulates the pursuit of the digitization of human activities *ad infinitum*, as the necessary condition for the development of the Internet in all directions. Therefore, the revolution in information technology is, perhaps, and for a long time to come, condemned to unfold only in those areas of human activity that are already operating in an "informational," although non-digital, form, as for exam-

---

[201] Dominique Wolton, cited by Sylvain Cypel, "Cybéria ou Cyberkeley, ou comment Internet peut anéantir ou favoriser les libertés," supplement to *Le Monde/L'Avenir, 2000-2099*.

ple all financial and accounting matters, which were the first to be computerized. Other areas seriously "resist" and probably will resist for a long time, as for example everything that has to do with human speech, which computers with good reason persistently fail to comprehend. The layers of information are therefore limited, and once everything that can be digitized has been (the last stage being the contents of our mediatized communications), the revolution will itself have run out of breath.

Even according to the strictly technical specifications, the actual development of the Internet appears to many to be rather conservative. Robert Cailliau, co-inventor of the "Web," does not hesitate to declare:

> Frankly speaking, I am a little disappointed. I do not think the Web is evolving rapidly. [...] At bottom, all informatics suffers from a stagnant paradigm. Computers get faster every day but there are hardly any new ideas: the architecture is always the same, as also the functionality.[202]

What some subjectively live as the beginning of a great permanent revolution is perhaps only the effect of the final maturation of a process now already some fifty years running.[203] It is true that the last stage of this process is the most visible and the most spectacular, since it concerns communications and social relations.

---

[202] Robert Cailliau, "Entretien: Internet et audiovisuel au-delà de la convergence," *Dossiers de l'audiovisuel*, no 8, INA, Paris, January-February 2000, p. 10.

[203] This coincides with the thesis of Alain Le Diberder, who explains in his last book (*Histoire d'@, op. cit.*) that the essential technological innovations at the base of the "Internet revolution" date from the seventies, themselves the culmination of the intuitions formulated twenty years before.

Some perverse effects of the new cult

Be that as it may, there are currently enough technical achievements in the area of communications—even if all progress were to stop today—to imagine that some perverse effects could temper the one-sided optimism of the "new globalists." Some promises risk being transformed into their opposites. Already, in the sixties, some forward-looking computer programmers, not without influence on their peers, were asking whether, paradoxically, the "change" would not be in a sense very conservative. Joseph Weizenbaum, of whom Lewis Mumford rightly said that he would "still [be] read in half a century," affirmed that "the computer, then, was used to conserve America's social and political institutions. It buttressed them and immunized them, at least temporarily, against enormous pressures for change."[204]

Many today fear that a "transparent" society would in fact become a "Big Brother" society, where the individual would have at his disposal only the narrowest margins of liberty. The promise of "more equality" generally made more attentive observers smile, for they noted the immense gulf between the rhetoric and the reality. We shall take as examples three already-apparent contradictions between the abstract promises and the facts. They concern the promise of "more power to the consumer," that of a more "collective" life, and that of "more equality." Many other promises could be scrutinized as well. They demonstrate that in the end the first steps toward the ideal world more often than not risk leading to regression rather than to progress.

A rolling back of liberties

There is no point in returning here to the oft-cited dangers that a society of Internet-for-everything could create for

---

[204] Joseph Weizenbaum, *Computer Power and Human Reason, op. cit.*, p. 31.

public liberties. We simply note that if these dangers are not visible it is because they are only "potential" in certain areas. Our liberal democratic societies have a velvet glove for what has to do with formal individual rights. The Internet on the other hand will systematically be a frightening tool in the iron hand of a non-democratic regime.

That potentiality is, moreover, already partly realized. We now know better the ambitions of the Echelon network, denounced in a European Parliament report.[205] In spite of the denials of the American government, the National Security Agency has been accused of indulging in systematically intercepting world communications, especially those traveling across the Internet. It seems that public opinion has not yet grasped the true measure of that vast spying enterprise. The Internet fundamentalists are caught in their own trap with their faith in the necessity of systematic transparence. Will they now also say that those who have nothing to hide have nothing to fear?

Liberties are equally threatened in a very real way by an unexpected development of the most brutal aspects of Internet commerce. That is the subject of the 1999 report of the *Commission nationale pour l'informatique et les libertés* (CNIL) in France, which was worried about the development of "cyber-surveillance" and the conditions of electronic commerce.

The bypassing of middlemen in commerce makes things very easy; too easy for some, like Solveig Godeluck, who notes that one need only click on an icon to go from decision to purchase to payment on-line: "The impulsive [shoppers] have an interest in self-policing."[206] The journalist notes the

---

[205] *Development of Surveillance Technology and Risk of Abuse of Economic Information*, STOA, Luxembourg. This report is composed of five different documents of which the one mentioned was edited by Duncan Campbell, the Scottish journalist who revealed the existence of the Echelon system in 1988.

[206] Solveig Godeluck, *Le boom de la netéconomie, op. cit.*, p. 122.

results of an American study that showed that in 1999, 25% of internauts said they were enticed by Internet advertising to make purchases, while only 14% of magazine readers and 11% of television viewers were.

The promise of "returning power" to the consumer appears to be very abstract in the face of the many attempts by Internet advertising companies to violate the private life of Internet users. The principle is simple and did not have to wait for new information technologies for its realization: the more the advertiser knows the life, tastes and habits of those addressed, the more he can adapt the message and increase the chances of seducing the viewer, and therefore of selling. Large American internet companies plant tracking devices onto the hard disks of the computers that connect to the Internet. These "cookies" allow them to follow the path of the consumer's Internet use completely legally, and to know their personal interests.

Some companies like Doubleclick, the largest of the type, have been accused of matching these facts with Web site user account records. The transparence is thus total. Everything happens in a context where the separation between the texts with "content," such as journalists' articles, book and CD reviews, and advertising copy is less and less clear. One need only look at an Internet service provider's page to see how especially fluid the borders are. That veritable goldmine, which is filled with the most extravagant fantasies of advertisers, is the origin of the fabulous stock quotes for all the Internet companies that capture the attention of the internauts. Expressing the point of view of many journalists, Éric Dupin sees a great danger,[207] that of an unprecedented manipulation of the consumer.

---

[207] Éric Dupin, "Mélange virtuel, danger réel. Sur le Net, la frontière entre information et publicité est de plus en plus ténue," *Libération*, 25 February 2000, p. 5.

The desynchronization of social activities

The hope of a more "collective" society appears, however, to be at odds with the desynchronization of social activities that the option of Internet-for-everything authorizes and encourages. The interactive character of relations in the world of the new information technologies repeats, with a strange insistence, what some have called the necessity of an "asynchronous" communication. This theme, present in outline in the text by Asimov, is markedly present in some recent proposals like those of Nicholas Negroponte. He insists that tomorrow, "Digital life will include very little real-time broadcast. [...] On-demand information will dominate digital life. We will ask explicitly and implicitly for what we want, when we want it."[208]

One of the projects of the director of the Media Lab at MIT focuses on portable digital interfaces, a kind of "personal assistant" that permits the individual to get all the information needed at the site where they are produced but by retrieving them whenever and in whatever form one chooses. For example, Negroponte imagines that

> There is another way to look at a newspaper, and that is as an interface to news. Instead of reading what other people think is news and what other people justify as worthy of the space it takes, being digital will change the economic model of news selections, make your interests play a bigger role, and, in fact, use pieces from the cutting-room floor that did not make the cut on popular demand. Imagine a future in which your interface agent can read every newswire and newspaper and catch every TV and radio broadcast on the planet, and then construct a personalized summary. This kind of newspaper is printed in an edition of one. [...] It would mix headline news with "less important'" stories relating to acquaintances, people you will see tomorrow, and

---

[208] Nicholas Negroponte, *Being Digital, op. cit.*, p. 168-169.

places you are about to go to or have just come from. It
would report on companies you know [...] Call it *The Daily
Me*.[209]

This wink to the French daily *Le Monde*[210] strikes one as
very curious in the context of a new social bond, where, if it
is understood correctly, one will never participate in a collective project that implies some kind of simultaneity, and one
will never again encounter the unexpected. Eric Klinenberg,
professor of sociology at the University of California, notes
in his analysis of the impoverishment of information on the
Internet that the network offers facts about the whole world
but that "in practice, the internauts use it only to amass information that touches them particularly. [...] It is a matter of
attracting at the same time a public egoistically turned toward
itself and the advertisers who want to get their attention."[211]

In this middle world, without surprise and without conflict, the virtual interactions unfold in a space where one is
always displaced in relation to the others. This is indeed very
far, in its reality, from the promises of finally doing away with
"human separation."

An increase of inequalities

There exist already—one cannot say still, since some of
them tend to increase—many inequalities in the area of access to communication and its basic techniques: reading and
argumentation. The revolution of printing is hardly finished.
Far from reducing the inequalities of access to learning we
may fear that the new world will develop towards the rein-

---

[209] *Ibid.*, p. 153.
[210] The French edition of Negroponte's book translates *The Daily Me* as
Mon monde.—tr.
[211] Éric Klinenberg, "Big city news ou l'information appauvrie," in Henry
Lelièvre (ed.), *Les États-Unis, maîtres du monde?* Complexe, Bruxelles, 1999, p.
107.

forcement of the already existing inequalities. The five million uneducated illiterates to be found in France already constitute a first crowd of those excluded from the system of learning. Those who are excluded from access, and above all from understanding the procedures necessary for the use of the new tools, risk being added to that number. The entire world is not naturally familiar with the turn of spirit which the new information technologies imply; and from this point of view, paradoxically, the schools do not make much effort to help the students acquire the basics of learning.

That fear is especially accented throughout the Third World. It is often said that the whole of Africa has fewer phone lines than New York or Tokyo. That permits us to measure the gap which risks becoming wider instead of being bridged over. We are very far from the talk about the "reunification of universal consciousness," and ever nearer to the classic situation of the growing domination of a few through their having mastered the tools that give power. It is more realistic to speak like Jean-Paul Fitoussi and Pierre Rosanvallon, of a "new age of inequalities."[212]

Indeed, it has been established that, on the whole, the creation of employment thanks to the new information technologies is not the El Dorado that was initially proclaimed. Serge Halimi, a *Monde diplomatique* journalist, remarked: "On the whole, fewer people work in information services and computers than in the three [major] supermarket chains."[213] The powerful Microsoft Corporation that weighs in on the stock exchange at several hundred billion dollars employs only 24,000 salaried employees. Certainly 90% of these are

---

[212] Jean-Paul Fitoussi and Pierre Rosanvallon, *Le nouvel âge des inégalités*, Seuil, Paris, 1996.
[213] Serge Halimi, "À propos du modèle américain," in Henri Lelièvre (ed.), *Les États-Unis, maîtres du monde?, op. cit.*, p. 50.

millionaires, but that only announces a profoundly unequal world.

Today no one truly contests that the rich are growing richer, that the income gap is increasing vertiginously and that, as the economist Alain Lipietz insists, the new information market leads to a breaking up of the middle classes.[214] The displacement of middlemen (many middle class professions function thus), which permits the Internet-for-everything, is, moreover, one of the factors essential to it. Above all there is the fear, as Erik Izraelewicz said, of the reinforcement of a "hyperclass," of an "elite spreading over the Internet who will dominate the world." These new cosmopolitans who are the only true "globalists" that have been known so far, live, according to Jacques Attali, in a "volatile society, indifferent to the future, egoistic and hedonistic, in fantasy and violence."[215]

The fantasy of the death of Man

The list of criticisms could go on. The promises are so numerous that it is almost certain that reality will resist. The neo-Buddhist kitsch poorly conceals the hard reality of the world. The hypothesis that a new Internet-for-everything society will come, as it is desired by the fundamentalists, is in fact very weak, not to say improbable. That is not where the problem lies. It is rather in the real, immediate effects that can result from clinging to this faith.

The Internet is, from this point of view, the Trojan Horse, full of profoundly anti-humanist values, shot through with the specter of the death of the human being. The new religiosity is, *stricto sensu*, a heresy of humanism. Its success rests

---

[214] Alain Lipietz, *La société en sablier*, La Découverte, Paris, 1998.
[215] Cited by Erik Izraelewicz, "Une hyperclasse? Quand une élite branchée sur Internet dominera le monde," supplement *Le Monde/L'Avenir, 2000-2099*.

upon a base of crisis, a crisis of values and of the social bond, recurring problems posed by never-ending destructive violence.

The cult of the Internet presents itself most often as an alternative to civilization, in the face of the old humanist values that have failed. The real difficulties of a changing global society also serve as a backdrop to the success of the new faith.

A success based on a crisis of values

As we have seen, the beliefs in information and transparency work a profound overturning of the order of values: The human being is no longer the master of this new religiosity, without center and without God; the individual consciousness is vulnerable to being "collectivized" and transferred to machines; the noosphere of cyberspace is substituted for the social and political organization of societies as we know them.

In fact, three essential values of the modern world are targeted here, all the more easily since they are moving through an unprecedented crisis of adaptation. These values, from historically different origins, are balanced in a provisional synthesis, both solid in its actual effects and at the same time fragile, since called to a necessary evolution.

In chronological order of appearance one can distinguish the monotheistic Jewish heritage of the Law, the importance given to speech (Logos) after the Athenian democratic revolution, and finally, clearly affirmed in the heart of the Christian world, the representation of the human being as an individual, endowed with interiority. These three themes—law, speech, and the individual—are being progressively detached from their original historical and geographical contexts to become, if not universal values, at least values claiming universality. It is no longer necessary to be a Jew of ancient Palestine to believe in the importance of law for regulating human affairs, no longer necessary to be a citizen of Athens or Syracuse to put speech and language at the center of human society, no longer necessary to be a Christian to see in man an inner free individual.

By becoming universal, these values have also become secular; that is to say, they have become detached from their religious and social substrata, in the sense that we accept that they transcend us. These three values have converged: the individual is the addressee of the law, and it is the individual alone who holds himself responsible before the law. The law is beyond the individual, yet it is the latter who makes the law through the collective play of language and the assembly of free individuals. The individual only exists in his speech, which proceeds equally from his inner memory and from the encounter with the speech of the Other.

This society of the law, of language and of the individual made a break with the ancient "holistic" society, to borrow the expression of the French anthropologist Louis Dumont, specialist in the history of individualism.[216] It is opposed to the belief in fate, in cycles, in organic inequalities, in private vengeance, and in caste systems that constituted—and still constitute—the temptation of social evolution. It nourished what we call "humanism."

The whole 20th century, that immense "Bluebeard's Castle" to borrow Steiner's phrase,[217] was a long hesitation to believe in the virtues of humanism. The crisis of confidence in the human being is immense, like the suspicion of political speech. As for the Law, it is doubly suspect of being in the service of the strong and of being in the end nothing but an

---

[216] Louis Dumont, *Essai sur l'individualism. une perspective anthropologique sur l'idéologie moderne*, Seuil, Paris, 1983. English translation: *Essays on Individualism: Modern Ideology in Anthropological Perspective*, University of Chicago Press, Chicago, 1986.
[217] George Steiner, *In Bluebeard's Castle: Some Notes Towards the Redefinition of Culture*, Yale University Press, New Haven, 1971.

unnecessary constraint. The cult of the Internet appears to nourish itself on an opposition to that foundational triptych of our modernity. Its success seems to be directly proportionate to that crisis of confidence.

The concrete effects of the attack on humanism

Whether the Internet continues in the direction that the fundamentalists seek to advance or not, the effects of an anti-humanist discourse are being felt no less in the present. Two fundamental representations are in the process of wavering before our eyes: that of being-together as relevant to life in society, and that of the human being as endowed with an unsurpassable singularity.

By force of repeating that the ideal life is one in which we would be separate, where direct encounter would be reduced to a rarity, the present, already-fragile social bond is threatened. The efforts of all those who try to teach men simply to "live in society" in order to be able to transform it in the common interest is undermined. What the Internet fundamentalists propose is nothing less than a progressive suppression of that life in society, in order to replace it with a simple "coexistence" for which there is no proof that it would be peaceful but for which all indications are that it would be conservative.

The Other finds himself always having a position in which he must obey the golden rule of interactive communication: Be there when I wish, in a form which I control and in that part of my territory to which I assign you. Sociality in the sense of mutuality disappears for the benefit of interactivity. The experience of the relation with the Other and with the world in general is replaced by virtual relations that are extremely reactionary, rapid and minimally engaging.

The fantasy of "cybersex" emanates from that instrumental vision at the very heart of that human activity which demands the greatest presence of the Other. (This was curiously put forward, with neither technology nor "tactile cybercombinations," in the film *Last Tango in Paris*, where the ideal of anonymous postmodern relations was carried to the extreme, to the point where one of the partners avows that now the best thing would be to "make love without touching.") We should not forget that pornography, that somber festival that sanctifies the absence of the Other, occupies a not-so negligible portion of the activity on the Internet. According to Michel Gensollen,

> Cybersex represents 25% of the traffic and a third of the requests on *Yahoo!*; one out of four internauts visits an adult site every day; this is the largest use at home (a fourth of the pages viewed) and the second largest use in the workplace (20% of pages viewed); 10% of electronic commerce today is X-rated.[218]

Incidentally, we should note that "sexual relations" with anonymous partners *via* the Internet, even though virtual, risks transgressing one of the fundamental prohibitions of civilization, that of incest. There is no way to tell if the anonymous partner at whatever distance is not a member of your own family...

It seems that a certain number of persons have already succumbed to that temptation to live henceforth alone in such a universe. According to some sociological studies, using the Internet tends, if one is not careful, to desocialize individuals. One study conducted in Pittsburg by Robert Kraut's team, followed 256 persons for two years and demonstrated that "greater use of the Internet was associated with declines in participants' communication with family members in the household, declines in the size of their social circle, and

---

[218] Michel Gensollen, "La création de valeur sur Internet," *loc. cit.* p. 23.

increases in their depression and loneliness."[219] A new type of solitary individual appears everywhere, one who maintains only informational and instrumental relations with the world around him. These "neo-mystics" construct a "social bond" that is no longer quite that of a human society.

This detachment of the human being from himself and from society paralyzes all impulse for change; instead that impulse is exhausted through technological change, which is the sole engine of evolution. One may fear that the global information society reveals itself completely spineless from the point of view of its capacity for transformation. Thus, the cult of the Internet is revealed to be a profoundly conservative impulse for civilization.

One other figure is on the way to being modified before our eyes: the representation of man as a human being. According to Sherry Turkle, we have for some years now witnessed a weakening of the metaphor of interiority for thinking about the individual, replacing it with the metaphor of the "program."[220] This American psychologist has observed that the traditional Freudian view of the unconscious, which had become the popular metaphor for interiority, became outdated in the North American world and was replaced by information metaphors. The animosity towards psychoanalysis goes along with the new cult of communication without interiority. The craze for postmodernism and the death of the subject completes this pessimistic scene.[221]

---

[219] Cited in *Sciences humaines*, no 108, August-September 2000, p. 10. The research report of Robert Kraut *et al.*, "Internet paradox: a social technology that reduces social involvement and psychological well-being?" is available on the web at: http://www.apa.org/journals/amp/amp5391017.html [English citation taken from the abstract on the web site.]

[220] Sherry Turkle, *The Second Self: Computers and the Human Spirit*, Simon and Schuster, New York, 1984.

[221] On this subject see: Céline Lafontaine, "La cybernétique, matrice du posthumanisme," *Cités*, PUF, Paris, septembre 2000.

The desire to detach consciousness from the body and at the same time to melt or "transfer" it into a transcendental collective threatens the delicate construction of the modern individual; and it accentuates the desire to detach oneself from the body as the latter constitutes the individual's identity.

Is the new cult immoral?

Behind this crisis of humanism, and combined with the attacks upon order brought along with this new faith, stands the question of the "death of Man." Not only is Man no longer a central figure, the true end of human society, but his disappearance is necessary in order to reach a higher stage of evolution. There, we are in the midst of the fantasy found in some scientific communities, in which Man is seen as a transformable being, able to be surpassed, a simple moment in the history of the world.

Is the cult of the Internet filled with an impulse towards death? Are the new information technologies in association with robotics, nanotechnologies and the genetic genie comparable, at worst, to the deadly potential of atomic physics? By pushing research in the direction of a "transfer of consciousness" from man into more intelligent robots, or of networks "endowed with life," do we not take the risk of making the human species disappear in so far as it is not adapted to this evolution?

This is the thesis put forth in a profoundly moving text by the American Bill Joy, one of the "fathers" of informatics and the inventor of Java software, who for a while presided over the American commission on the future of research in information technologies. That text, published in *Wired* in April 2000, generated reactions around the world. It is the fruit of a twinge of conscience of a researcher up to now an admirer of technical progress and ardent contributor to it, getting from it, as he himself said, a "feeling of peace."

His conclusion is sobering:

> My continuing professional work is on improving the reliability of software. Software is a tool, and as a toolbuilder I must struggle with the uses to which the tools I make are put. I have always believed that making software more reliable, given its many uses, will make the world a safer and better place; if I were to come to believe the opposite, then I would be morally obligated to stop this work. I can now imagine such a day may come. This all leaves me not angry but at least a bit melancholic. Henceforth, for me, progress will be somewhat bittersweet.[222]

The main fear of Bill Joy, who seems to have suddenly seen death prowling in the place where up until now peace and optimism about the future of these technologies had reigned, concerns precisely "our chances of remaining ourselves and likewise of remaining human beings" in such a world, because of the progress in "auto-reproductive" techniques. The computer programmer appears ready because of that to renounce what is, as we have seen, one of the fundamental values of this milieu:

> We have, as a bedrock value in our society, long agreed on the value of open access to information, and recognize the problems that arise with attempts to restrict access to, and development of, knowledge. [...] But despite the strong historical precedents, if open access to and unlimited development of knowledge henceforth puts us all in clear danger of extinction, then common sense demands that we reexamine even these basic, long-held beliefs.[223]

---

[222] Bill Joy, "Why the future doesn't need us," *Wired*, issue 8.04, April 2000. 11p. http://www.wired.com/wired/archive/8.04/joy.html
[223] *Ibid.*

Is the new cult of the Internet immoral? This is, indeed, at bottom, the question that those who have been the great architects of informatics have repeatedly posed from the inside, from Norbert Wiener to Joseph Weizenbaum to Bill Joy. If one takes sides with humanity, the fear arises that the response to that question cannot be entirely positive. The debate should not, then, leave indifferent all those who, well beyond the Internet, are attached to humanist values.

Bibliography

Alberganti, Michel. *Le Monde* 26 May 1999: 29.

Arsac, Jacques. *Les machines à penser.* Paris: Seuil, 1987.

Asimov, Isaac. *Naked Sun.* New York: Ballantyne, 1983.

Ballard, J.G. *"The intensive care unit." Myths of the Near Future.* London: Jonathan Cape, 1982.

Bell, Daniel. *The Coming of Post-Industrial Society. A Venture in Social Forecasting.* New York: Basic Books, 1973.

Belot, Laure, and Enguérand Renault. "Les attaques sur le Net ébranlent la nouvelle économie." *Le Monde* 11 Feb. 2000.

Blanchard, Sandrine. "Le premier marché mondial de l'éducation s'est ouvert à Vancouver." *Le Monde* 26 May 2000.

Bosquet, Annie, and Philippe Breton. "La place des personnes âgées dans l'argumentaire et le discours d'accompagnement des nouvelles technologies de communication." *Rapport de recherche MIRE-CNAV* Mar. 1998.

Breton, Philippe. *À l'image de l'homme. Du golem aux créatures virtuelles.* Paris: Seuil, 1996.
---. *La parole manipulée.* Paris: La Découverte, 1998.

---. *La tribu informatique. Enquête sur une passion moderne.* Paris: Métailié, 1990.
---."Le premier ordinateur copiait le cerveau humain." *Recherche* 290 Sep. 1996.
---."L'informaticien et la sécurité: enquête sur un antago-nism." *Les cahiers de la sécurité intérieure* 1996.
---."L'oubli de la tortue." *Alliages* 1991.
---. *L'utopie de la communication.* Paris: La Découverte/Poche, 1997.

Bureau, Jacques. *L'ère logique.* Paris: Robert Laffont, 1969.

Cailliau, Robert. De Gutenberg ao terceiro milénio, Universi-dad autonoma de Lisboa. 6-8 Apr. 2000
---."Entretien: Internet et audiovisuel au-delà de la conver-gence." *Dossiers de l'audiovisuel* 8 (2000): 10.

Cypel, Sylvain. "Cybéria ou Cyberkeley, ou comment Internet peut anéantir ou favoriser les libertés."*Le Monde/L'Avenir* 2000-2099: supplement.

De garis, Hugo. "Fracture idéologique." *Le Monde interactif* 5 July 2000.

Dery, Mark. *Vitesse virtuelle. La cyberculture aujourd'hui.* Paris: Abbeville, 1997.

Duclos, Denys. *Le complexe du loup-garou. la fascination de la vio-lence dans la culture américaine.* Paris: La Découverte, 1994.

Dumont, Louis. *Essai sur l'individualism. une perspective anthro-pologique sur l'déologie modern.* Paris: Seuil, 1983.
---. *Essays on Individualism: Modern Ideology in Anthropological Per-spective.* Chicago: U of Chicago, 1986.

Dupin, Eric. "Mélange virtuel, danger réel. Sur le Net, la frontière entre information et publicité est de plus en plus ténue." *Libération* 25 Feb 2000: 5.
---. Rev. of Le cult de l'Internet: une menace pour le lien social? Philippe Breton. World Press Review 1991 v.16, nr.1 p.161-2.

Dupuy, Jean-Pierre. *Aux origines des sciences cognitive.* Paris: La Découverte, 1992.

Ellul, Jacques. *La technique ou l'enjeu du siècle.* Paris: Armand Colin, 1954.
---. *Le bluff technologique.* Paris: Hachette, 1988.
---.*The Technological Bluff.* Grand Rapids: Eerdmans, 1990.
---. *The Technological Society.* New York: Knopf, 1964.

Eudes, Yves. *Le Monde* 28 Apr. 2000: 16-17.
---.*Le Monde* 29 May 2000: 37.

European Parliament. *Development of Surveillance Technology and Risk of Abuse of Economic Information,* Luxembourg: STOA, 2000.

Falque-Pierrotin, Isabelle. "Quelle régulation pour Internet et les réseaux?" *Le Monde, Horizons-Débats* 27 Nov. 1999

Fitoussi, Jean-Paul, and Pierre Rosanvallon. *Le nouvel âge des inégalités.* Paris: Seuil, 1996.

Flichy, Patrice. "Internet ou la communauté scientifique idéale." *Réseaux* 97 (1999).
---. *The Internet Imaginaire.* Cambridge: MIT, 2007.

Gates, Bill. *The Road Ahead.* New York: Viking, 1995.

Gensollen, Michel. "La création de valeur sur Internet." *Réseaux* 97 (1999): 63-64.

Gibson, William. *Neuromancer.* New York: Ace, 1984.

Godeluck, Solveig. *Le boom de la netéconomie. Comment Internet bouleverse les règles du jeu économique.* Paris: La Découverte, 2000.

Gore, Al. Remarks as delivered by Vice President Al Gore to the Superhighway Summit, UCLA. 11 Jan. 1994. Available at: http://clinton1.nara.gov/White_House/EOP/OVP/other/superhig.html

Gras, Alain and Sophie Poirot-Delpech. *Grandeur et dépendance, sociologie des macrosystèmes techniques.* Paris: PUF, 1993.

Guédon, Jean-Claude. *La planète cyber. Internet et le cyberspace.* Gallimard coll. Paris: Découvertes, 1996.

Gusdorf, George. *La parole.* Paris: PUF, 1952.

Habermas, Jürgen. *Technik und Wissenschaft als "Ideologie,".* Suhrkamp, 1968.

Heims, Steve. *John Von Neumann and Norbert Wiener.* Cambridge: MIT, 1982.

Hiltz, Roxanne, and Murray Turoff. *The Network Nation: Human Communication via Computer.* Cambridge: MIT, 1993.

Hodges, Alan. *Alan Turing: the Enigma.* London: Vintage, 1992.

Huitema, Christian. *Et Dieu créa Internet.* Paris: Eyrolles, 1996.

Izraelewicz, Erik. "Une hyperclasse? Quand une élite branchée sur Internet dominera le monde." *Le Monde/L'Avenir* 2000-2099: supplement.

Joy, Bill. "Why the future doesn't need us." *Wired* 8.04 Apr 2000. http://www.wired.com/wired/archive/8.04/joy.html.

Kapor, Mitchell. "Where is the digital highway really heading?" *Wired* 1.03 July-Aug. 1993.

Lafontaine, Céline. *Cybernétique et sciences humaines: aux origines d'une représentation informationnelle du sujet.* Montréal: U of Montréal, 2001.

Lapouge, Gilles. *Utopie et civilizations.* Paris: Albin Michel, 1990.

Le Breton, David. *L'adieu au corps.* Paris: Métailié, 1999.

Lefebvre, Henri. *Position: contre les technocrats.* Paris: Méditations, 1967.

Lelièvre, Henry. *Les États-Unis, maîtres du monde?* Brussels: Complexe, 1999.

Lévy, Pierre. *World philosophie.* Paris: Odile Jacob, 2000.

Licklider, J.C.R. and Robert W. Taylor. "The computer as a communication device." *Science and Technology* Apr. 1968: 21.

Lipietz, Alain. *La société en sablier.* Paris: La Découverte, 1998.

Lyotard, Jean-François. *La Condition Postmoderne.* Paris: Minuit, 1979.

---. *The Postmodern Condition: a Report on Knowledge.* Minneapolis: U of MN.

Madelin, Alain. "L'opposition contre la 'Bové Pride'." *Le Monde* 2-3 July 2000: 6.

Magloire, Georges, and Hubert Cuypers. *Teilhard de Chardin.* Paris: Éditions universitaires, 1964.

Mandard, Stéphane. "La vie rêvée des domoticiens." *Le Monde interactif* 2 Feb. 2000.

Martin, Graham. "Interview." Libération 29-30 Jan. 1994.

Mattelart, Armand. *Histoire de l'utopie planétaire. De la cité prophétique à la société globale.* Paris: La Découverte, 1999.
---. "L'âge de l'information. Genèse d'une appellation non controlee." *Hermès Science Publications* 101 (2000).
---. *The Information Society: An Introduction.* London: Sage, 2001.

McLuhan, Marshall. *The Gutenberg Galaxy: The Making of Typographic Man.* Toronto: U of Toronto, 1962.

Morange, Michel. *Histoire de la biologie moléculaire.* Paris: La Découverte, 1994.

Mortaigne, Véronique, and Nicole Vurser. "La difficile défense des droits d'auteur sur Internet." *Le Monde* 31 May 2000: 23

Musso, Pierre. *Télécommunications et philosophie des réseaux. La postérité paradoxale de Saint-Simon.* Paris: PUF, 1997.

Negroponte, Nicholas. *Being Digital.* New York: Knopf, 1995.

Neveu, Erik. *Une société de communication?* Paris: Montchrestien, 1997.

Nivelle, Pascale. Libération 25 Feb. 2000.

Pirsig, Robert. *Zen and the Art of Motorcycle Maintenance.* New York: William Morrow, 1999.

Pörksen, Uwe. *Plastic words.* University Park: Penn State U, 1995.

Puech, Henri-Charles. "Manichéisme" *Encyclopaedia universalis.*

Quéau, Philippe. De Gutenberg ao terceiro milénio, Universidad autonoma de Lisboa. 6-8 Apr. 2000.
---. *Le virtuel, virtues et vertiges.* Seysel: Champ-Vallon, 1993.

Ramonet, Ignacio. *La tyrannie de la communication.* Paris: Galilée, 1999.

Reding, Viviane, and Nicole Vurser. "Interview with Nicole Vurser." *Le Monde* 31 May 2000: 23.

Renault, Enguérand. *Le Monde* 4 Mar. 2000: 23

Roszak, Theodore. *The Cult of Information.* New York: Pantheon,1986.

Science et synthèse. Paris: Gallimard/Unesco, 1967.

Segal, Howard. *Technological Utopianism in American Culture.* Chicago: U of Chicago, 1985

Sfez, Lucien. *Critique de la communication.* Paris: Seuil, 1988.
---. *La santé parfaite.* Paris: Le Seuil, 1995.

---. *Quaderni* 40 (1999-2000): 7.

Sloterdijk, Peter. "Le centrisme mou au risque de penser." *Le Monde* 9 Oct. 1999.

Steiner, George. *In Bluebeard's Castle: Some Notes Towards the Redefinition of Culture*. New Haven: Yale UP, 1971.

Takeshi, Ozaki. *Courrier International* Jul. 1994.

Tardieu, Michel, and Pierre Hadot. "Gnose" *Encyclopaedia universalis*.

Teilhard de Chardin, Pierre. *Le phénomène humain*. Paris: Seuil, 1955.
---. *The Phenomenon of Man*. New York: Harper, 1959.

Ternisien, Xavier. "Les religions sont entrées en force sur Internet." *Le Monde* 9-10 July 2000.

Tincq, Henri. "La métamorphose de Dieu." *Le Monde/L'Avenir* 2000-2099: Supplement.

Toffler, Alvin. *The Third Wave*. New York: Morror, 1980.

Trigano, Shmuel. *Le monothéisme est un humanisme*. Paris: Odile Jacob, 2000.

Truong, Jean-Michel. *Le successeur de Pierre*. Paris: Denoël, 1999.

Turing, Alan. "Les ordinateurs et l'intelligence." in *Pensée et machine*, Champ-Vallon: Seysel, 1983.

Turkle, Sherry. *The Second Self: Computers and the Human Spirit*. New York: Simon and Schuster, 1984.

Vattimo, Gianni. *The Transparent Society*. Baltimore: Johns Hopkins UP, 1992.

Vedel, Thierry. "Les politiques des autoroutes de l'information dans les pays industrialisés: une analyse comparative." *Réseaux* 78. (1996): 11-25.

Virilio, Paul. *L'art du moteur*. Paris: Galilée, 1993.
---. *The Art of the Motor*. Minneapolis: 1995.

Weizenbaum, Joseph. *Computer Power and Human Reason: from Judgment to Calculation*. San Francisco: W.F. F Freeman: 1976.

Wiener, Norbert. *The Human Use of Human Beings: Cybernetics and Society*. 2nd ed. New York: Doubleday Anchor, 1956.

Wolton, Dominique. , "Cybéria ou Cyberkeley, ou comment Internet peut anéantir ou favoriser les libertés." *Le Monde/L'Avenir* 2000-2099: Supplement.
---. *Internet et après? Une théorie critique des nouveaux medias*. Paris: Flammarion, 2000.

Wunenburger, Jean-Jacques. "Regard et transparence, utopie et philosophie." *Quaderni* 40 (1999-2000): 153.

Young, Jeffrey S. *Steve Jobs: the Journey is the Reward*. Glenview: Foresman, 1988.

Index